SOUL PU

This book is dedicated
to the unfolding of personal consciousness
towards and within
the oneness of life.

SOUL
PURPOSE
ASTROLOGY

How to read your birth chart for growth and transformation

Margaret Koolman

Davies & Ritchie

D&R

Published by Davies & Ritchie
14 Tyndale Park, Herne Bay, Kent CT6 6BP, UK

First published 1998.

ISBN: 0-9534270-0-5

Printed in Great Britain by
Whitstable Litho Ltd.

ACKNOWLEDGEMENTS

I am deeply and gratefully indebted to Maureen Ritchie, my gentle editor, for her kind and incisive suggestions and corrections of the manuscript. Her philosophical questioning drew out my understanding and helped me to express it. Her encouragement and happy sharing of my excitement at every stage has made the creation of this book a joy.

I wish to thank also my son Howard Koolman, who shares my interests as a friend and wrote the astrology software that enables me to maintain my own individual style of chart reading; my son Adrian Koolman, who manages me with understanding and tact and faithfully reproduced my diagrams on the computer; my friend and supportive rock, Graham Davies, who has consistently provided organisation, stability, space and acceptance whenever needed.

There are too many dear and helpful people in my life to name them all but I would like to mention Liz Poole, Nancy Kidder and Sandra Lee, who provided the necessary validation, space and encouragement for me to write the first draft in Hawaii; Jennifer Day, editor and writer, who helped me to believe that my work was worth publishing; Lief Bruylant, artist, who shares my excited enthusiasm for life and helped in the final stages of book production; and David Cousins, healer, whose lantern lights my path.

I wish to thank those dear friends and supporters all over the world, who have provided me with shelter and work for the last three years; and my astrology students and clients, who have given me 'grist for the mill' since my astrological career began 23 years ago; and thank you Bernard Honey, my first teacher, for telling me to practice first and read later.

Contents

Preface		
Introduction		1
Chapter 1	**Overview**	13
	The Centre of the Circle	
	We are the same only different	
	Logic and Intuition	
	Astrology in a Nutshell	
	Transformative Chart Reading	
Chapter 2	**The Zodiac**	
	Part 1 *Ways in which we are the same*	27
	The 4 elements making the 12 Zodiac Signs	
	The Zodiac as 12 pieces of a process - the Seasons	
	The Zodiac as 12 pieces of a personality	
	The Zodiac Story	
	Part 2 *Ways in which we are different*	64
	Tropical vs Sidereal Zodiac - a bit of astronomy	
	Each Sign has its difficulty	
	Negative opposites to Sun-Signs	
Chapter 3	**The Planets**	
	Part 1 *Ways in which we are the same*	77
	The 'Seven Sacred Planets' as chakras	
	Planets as human characteristics in personal development + chart meanings	
	How the planets rule the Zodiac Signs	
	"Why the planets were formed" - a story	

Part 2 Ways in which we are different 105
The relationship of planets to each other -
'Aspects' described in full
A list of Aspects in Brief (with exercises)
The seven 'chakra' planets in a birth chart -
in Signs and aspect with examples
Outer planets in aspect to the inner seven
Chiron
We are not separate from Spirit

Chapter 4 **The Houses**
Part 1 Ways in which we are the same 149
A bit of astronomy - the physical Houses
The 12 Houses through which we experience
Creating our experience

Part 2 Ways in which we are different 158
The Ascendent
The Descendent and relationship
The 12 Houses:
How we create our experience
How our experience reflects our personality
Planets in Houses
Ruling planets of 'empty' Houses
Looking beyond the 'windows'

Chapter 5 **The Nodes of the Moon**
Part 1 Ways in which we are the same 183
Our story
Off the path and getting back on
The 12 directions

Part 2 Ways in which we are different 199
Ruling planets of the Nodes
Aspects to the Nodes
A personal path through life

Conclusion 207

Preface

I discovered that my grandmother had been an astrologer when I received some of her books from my father after she had died. At the time I was studying the great philosophers of the past and discovering the dubious pleasure of finding flaws in other people's thinking. I was a cynic and I determined to find the flaws in astrology also. I knew that to bring any system down, one needs to study it first and the weaknesses reveal themselves to the discerning mind, so I studied astrology at a basic level and began to practise the principles through the charts of my friends.

I discovered that I could find out things about them that they had never told before, and I realised that, whatever flaws there may be, astrology actually works. For me at that point, 'the Earth shook' and I stopped bothering to try disproving philosophies and started the great and joyful exploration of understanding myself and other people.

A birth chart reading can be a wonderful, enlightening and opening experience. At best, the recipient of such a reading gains a sense of complete acceptance, of doors opening to endless possibilities, of previous emotional painfulness becoming positive hopeful experience, and of the relief, both of finding themself, and also feeling recognized by the universe.

As I see it, life is about fulfilling our part in the evolutionary process, which we do naturally when we give to life, and we give most when we follow that course which brings us the fullest sense of satisfaction on all levels. In order to consciously search out that course, we need to know our personality fairly well, and to be aware of, and appreciate, our abilities and skills.

I find that I also need to accept my difficulties with life, my knee-jerk reactions and recurring problems. Not to accept them weakens my sense of personal value, but at the same time I must also realize that they are probably out of date and no longer relevant.

For me, understanding the positive principles of Zodiac Signs, planets and Houses, is invaluable. In the birth chart we can read our character, and see what tasks and activities our particular talents might suggest. We can also read the difficulties, and, through a spiritual philosophy, we might also see how they came about, and how to move beyond them by adjusting our attitudes.

I think of the soul as that part of us which can never be happy without the touch of spirit. The soul draws from the personality the finer expressions of human nature in order to fulfil its purpose which is to reach and blend with spirit. Soul Purpose Astrology is about refining the personality so that this purpose can be achieved, creating the gift of spiritual Light in and through Earth experience.

This philosophical view leads me to a greater sense of self-acceptance and, with the subsequent relaxation from anxiety and guilt, I become able to allow myself to follow my sense of purpose, that deep knowledge of what feels right for me to do, which is expressed by 'the Nodes of the Moon' in my chart.

Anyone wanting to understand their own and others' lives better through their birth charts will find here the basic information they need in order to start unfolding character and experience in a positive growthful way. There is always, of course, much more that could be said at every stage, but understanding it *all* is not necessary.

Much basic knowledge can be immediately applied to the people we know. If a friend has been fumbling in uncertainty or depression, simply knowing their Zodiac Sun-Sign gives us a tool to help them get back to their centre (see 'Negative Opposite Signs' in the chapter on the Zodiac).

When a reading is insensitively given, it can be a shock and leave a person doubtful of their value and apprehensive about the future. Such impressions can be alleviated and dispersed by a vision of our place within the whole, and the realization that every lesson in life can be negative or positive depending entirely upon whether one's attitude to life is of 'a glass half empty' or 'a glass half full': closed and protective, or open and growing.

The Introduction of this book begins with a philosophical approach to the whole of life which is not, in itself, part of astrological principles, but rather underlies the way I apply those principles to the questions of 'how?' and 'why?' about our life as part of existence as a whole. It is not essential to read the Introduction first, and a beginner in astrology might prefer to start with 'Astrology in a Nutshell' in Chapter 1, or 'the Story of the Zodiac' in Chapter 2.

Throughout the book the principles of Zodiac Signs, planets and Houses will be presented many times in different ways. Looking from different perspectives, a fuller picture gradually emerges, replacing a beginner's confusion with greater and greater clarity.

It is not the purpose of this book to give descriptions of every planet in every Sign and House. Rather, the basic principles are explored, and the method of using them for positive benefit is demonstrated with many examples.

There are exercises given at many points, encouraging the reader to think about experience from different directions. Many of these exercises consist of questions, and as every person is different, there will be many different ways of answering them. All answers that you come up with are valid for you. The questions are designed as a process which will draw out both your inner knowledge of what is right for you, and your intuitions for others.

Even a little understanding, wisely used, can be valuable. Like a small torch in the dark, it may not show the entire scene at a glance, but it can save you from tripping over your less useful habits, and possibly even help you see where you are going.

Introduction

The most significant personal moment, in terms of our life as spirit on Earth, is the moment of birth, the birth of our own separate, individually tailored set of equipment, our earthly body. As spirit, we had been hovering around the body of the mother, gathering this foetus as a set of faculties, or tools, for perceiving and interpreting our experience, and at some point commiting ourself to the coming life.

At the moment of birth, this little body is cut loose from the womb, that reminder of universal Oneness. The threshold is crossed and our earthly experience begins: the quality of that beginning is reflected in everything around us.

Beginnings set the scene for what follows so if we map the heavens at the birth moment of any person, group or project, we can learn something of the context and qualities to be unfolded. These maps are two-dimensional charts of the three-dimensional universe, and 'astrology' is the interpretation, according to specific principles, of charts drawn for significant moments of time.

Everything in the world around us reflects us, and the world is moving, changing and reacting, as we are ourselves. The only movement that is regular and predictable is that of the 'celestial lights'. So, looking at the chart of a chosen moment can give reliable feedback, and the system of meaning used has been established over many hundreds of years. Generally, the celestial lights astrologers choose to chart are the sun, moon and planets; sometimes distant stars and galaxies are included as are certain asteroids. The belt of sky that contains the sun, moon and planets is divided into twelve Zodiac Signs to define planetary positions.

To the person viewing the heavens, its appearance at any moment can express that moment entirely; it shows us a pattern, or matrix, that relates to every aspect of that moment in every dimension in which experience is possible, from our spiritual source through to the appearance of the physical world around us. The pattern of our birth chart represents the matrix of our life as a separate being, and can be interpreted at any level.

So, every dimension of a person's experience can be found in their birth chart, and the particular interpretation given depends on the level of focus of the interpreter.

For the physical level of a reading, an astrologer refers to the planets as indicators of events, people in our lives and the state of our physical body. The twelve divisions of the circle from the Earth point of view, called Houses, represent areas of daily life; for instance, career is seen in the 10th House which is the highest part of the sky at the top of the chart, earnings are seen in the 2nd House, partnership in the 7th.

On the level of vital energy, the pattern of planetary energies shows our health through the organisation of our energy system, and shows what experience we attract through the energy we give out.

On the emotional level we read, through the chart, about emotional reactions and tendencies. Who or what sparks them off can be suggested by using the Houses.

On the mental level we are dealing more with attitudes: assumed and often unconscious, or learned, cultivated characteristics.

On a soul level, we are looking at the highest potential of the characteristics shown by the planetary arrangement, and our chosen purpose for this particular life. Spiritually, we can regard each planet as representing an archetypal energy principle of human life, and the Zodiac itself as twelve faces of God in human form shining through the human heart; each life our spirit chooses one Sun Sign as the quality of human heart through which to radiate.

Almost the whole of our conscious experience is of Time unfolding. There can be moments, between heart-beats, when we recognise the eternal infinity of timelessness, but normally we each relate to our world through the varied vibrations of our own personal senses. Each conscious experience we have elicits a response, an internal action, and this is likely to become an unconscious reaction in later circumstances that appear to us the same. What has happened before, we expect to happen again and we prepare ourselves for it.

We each read the world in our own way, actually perceiving what we have come to expect and reacting to it again. Within Time, we experience many lifetimes as individual forms and every lifetime adds to our accumulation of expectations. The result is that we interpret most of what we see in terms of these conditioned expectations, and so the surroundings that we perceive are reflecting that conditioning back to us. The spirit that we are has very little chance of interfering in all this; sometimes, even when we suspect that things may be different from what they seem to be, we have great difficulty in not reacting in the same old way.

However, when we are in touch with our spiritual self, we can see clearly because in truth it is all spirit anyway; our spiritual light reflected in the world shows us a vision of completeness, deep value, true meaning, where the reality of Oneness shines through diversity, on one level dissolving it. One way to be in touch with these clear reflections of spirit is to become familiar with those reactions and responses of ours that obscure them. As we become aware of the extent to which our life experience is due to our personality perspective, we realise that we ourselves are clouding what we are looking at. When we look again with that in mind, the way is open for that clear vision, and we can consciously recognise that all things are truly spirit.

Ways of looking at birth charts

It is very important to be aware that we are not formed or affected by our birth chart, any more than land is formed or affected by a map we may draw of its features. Our birth chart can be interpreted as a map of the world the way we personally tend to understand it. In giving us a picture of our personal way of perceiving our life, the chart confirms our experience. We may also realise that things may be different for others which will be seen from their birth charts. This confirmation of our personal experience helps us to know and accept our personality as it is, and it is our greater, or higher, self that is doing the accepting - the personality is not all we are.

Just by looking at our birth chart, we take the position of observer. The emotional clinging to experience drops away for a moment, revealing a clearer vision of ourselves as spirit clothed in personality. In relationships, once we realise the extent of our assumptions about other people, we can start to wonder who they really are and relate to them directly.

One way we can use our birth chart is to help us locate our negative attitudes and feelings. As we begin to understand them, the aspect of our character which has defended itself with them reveals to us its essential virtues, and they can then be integrated. Another way we can use the chart is to focus on our positive potential so that we grow more consciously into all that we can be, rather than giving energy to our habitual smallness. A third way, on receiving the astrological confirmation of our personality structure, is to identify ourselves with the higher self and let the spirit shine through that personality, which naturally brings out its best.

Astrology can help us develop tolerance and understanding of people by showing us how very different our personalities are. Our birth charts give clues as to what the differences are and how the consequent experiences feel; they are like mirrors of our individual personality. As you would look in the glass to see if your hair is as you wish it, or check that there is no cabbage leaf round your teeth from lunch, so you can look into your astrological birth chart to check whether you are 'being yourself' or are caught in some role left over from past pressures, like the need to survive, be successful, or conform.

Through your chart, you can check the accuracy of your empathic intuition, finding whether it works better for you to trust responses from your mind, your heart or your solar plexus; and you can find out in which circumstances you are liable to make mistakes.

You can also work out your best career, given your personality's particular talents and skills, and discover whether that career will really give you all the satisfaction you want, or whether you also need a more personal form of service.

You can see how you choose behaviour in accordance with your expectations of other people's motives and opinions, and how that creates the experience you have with those people, and with the world at large. If your relationships tend to have similar outcomes, you can discover why.

Children - the process of birth

When you look into the mirror of a child's personality, you will know better what kind of encouragement to give. As well as being similar in many ways, children have very different personalities from each other from the first moments of life. There are so many combinations possible of all the information that makes up a birth chart, that the only time two people will have the same combination is when they are born at the same time in the same place. Even with twins born within moments of each other, those few minutes make a difference. Comparisons of people born at similar times but not brought up together, show many identical timings of events, coincidences of names, and other odd similarities but basically they are still different people.

Children have their basic character potential around them from before birth and a predisposition to react to their parents a certain way, all of which can be seen in their birth chart. Yet they also have their inheritance of genes and DNA, and the upbringing that will occur due to the parents' life circumstances and experience (like the degree of financial wealth, and the nationality), and these things cannot be seen astrologically.

Between lives, although we still continue to identify individually, we withdraw from the vision of material separation and so it is easier to see that separation is ultimately not real. Many spirits are drawn to create physicality again through the desire for some experience they remember; and some come into the physical dimension with the purpose of maintaining the spiritual perspective and the desire to help other people do the same. Perhaps we are pulled into, or choose, earthly life at a particular time for our spirit to fulfil the needs of that time and of those parents. There are as many purposes as there are people and, although a birth chart shows an enormous amount about a person, it cannot show the individual spirit.

As spirit creating a life of earthly experience, we choose those abilities which will help us to fulfil this life's purpose. We have a vast fund of experiences from the past through which we have developed those abilities but, in the lives where they were developed, we will have had difficulties that were not solved and relationships that needed balancing, together with attitudes and habits which are not necessarily relevant to this life, and all that must come with the chosen abilities. So our particular blend of characteristics may not be what we would consciously choose from our present relatively limited viewpoint.

As our spirit extends itself, the physical, emotional and mental conditions of our particular parents and upbringing are attracted through the vibration of our purpose and the character it requires; the incoming vibration is creating the earthly circumstances that receive it. The new baby, when responding to each experience, draws on the qualities and programming that its spirit has brought, and this pulls the personality into incarnation piece by piece.

These responses are not necessarily being chosen because they work in the moment; sometimes they do not work well at all, but they are part of the pre-existing equipment. Sometimes a child appears to over-react to some minor situation; this may be due to the situation triggering a memory of a time long past, and the reaction is to that time rather than the present. Its personality is reflected in every part of the baby's world; the genes, the DNA, the lines of the palm, the surrounding people, and many other mirrors of life - and the birth chart maps the pattern of it all.

Looking at the birth chart of their child can help a parent be more understanding of the child's behaviour.

Children need to be the way they are, true to their feelings in the moment. Any child will benefit if we can help them use their set of characteristics with more awareness and skill, but if we try to change their basic character we are simply burying the tools they need to fulfil their spirit's purpose. As parents, being part of the picture that will develop the child's character, we too need to be what we are to the best of our ability, accepting ourselves kindly, so that they also learn to be accepting. In this way we can assist the unfolding of our child's potential in the best possible way for them.

Partnership

Another area of life where an informed look at birth charts can be helpful, is partnership. Every individual person you relate to also has a birth chart. That is to say, their spirit chose a set of characteristics before coming to earth. They, too, have an ideal to work for, an aim to achieve, a purpose to discover, which may be very different from your own. Their survival behaviour at birth would have been in accordance with their personality 'tool kit', and their predisposition will have created their particular experiences and decisions about life. All these may not coincide with yours, even though you may be very attracted to them.

From the planetary positions at this person's birth, we can see the chosen character and what their path through life may be about. Comparing your chart and theirs can indicate what connections there may be between you. The problems can be clearly seen, and therefore focused on in a constructive way. The chemistry of day to day living is complex and may seem insoluble unless we can step back into our 'observer' and get a more detached look at what is going on. Astrology can give that detached view.

Play with astrology

The language of astrology is written in symbols. A symbol is like a doorway. Even within different philosophies, the meanings given to a very basic symbol will tend to be similar. Basic symbols are part of the structure of life itself, so quietly contemplating a symbol, or combination of symbols, can bring realisations about the aspect of life being represented.

All that is written about astrology is basically what different people have learned through contemplating and playing with astrological symbols, and applying their learning to whatever area of life interests them, be it human character, world events, answers to questions, or timings of events. If you would like to contemplate the symbols of astrology yourself, you will find that your understanding of the basic principles will be enhanced.

One can play with the ideas in astrology, just enjoying the astrological way of viewing life. It can be quite exciting to see for the first time which Zodiac sign Mercury was travelling through, or transiting, when you were born. At last here is a reflection of the way your mind works and the kind of things you communicate about most easily. This can describe, amongst other things, why certain areas of experience fascinate you and others do not interest you at all, or may be difficult to understand. It will show your particular needs in any learning situation.

Venus reflects the way we relate to people and in what kind of surroundings we feel good. Many of us tend to model our expectations of communication and relationship on the behaviour accepted by society or our group. This behaviour may work for some, but it is not necessarily the best way for everybody. Other people choose behaviour out of *their* 'tool kit'; ours may be very different. So, when we see which sign Venus was transiting at our birth, we may recognise at last, that something important to us personally has been missing from our relationships. Accepting that, we can start behaving in a way that will attract it into our relationships in future.

When we examine our birth chart, the confirmation of our character and inner direction helps us to release our potential. Accepting ourselves, we begin to hear, and give credence to, our own inner guidance.

If we could learn to totally accept ourselves and unconditionally love all our experience, there would be no need for personal exploration of our make-up, our earthly equipment; we would blend with Oneness and the need for a personality would disappear. When we have difficulty with such complete acceptance, knowing how we function can help us understand and deal with the habitual pitfalls of our particular personality, and also help us believe in and use our finer qualities. Bringing assumptions and expectations into consciousness is the beginning of retrieving the power they seem to have over our behaviour; we start to realise that we make our own lives, and so can choose to do it differently. This makes it easier for each of us to be the open, loving soul we truly are.

Our experience of life is what is true for us. A birth chart shows us a map of life experience but not the experiences themselves. We get a more complete and detailed view of ourselves and what we are doing, from what seems to be happening around us, reflecting us from many angles.

Although astrology can be used in many ways, a chart is only as useful as its interpreter makes it. It should therefore never be the last word in any situation. Before decisions are made in life, there is a need to look at the whole of our world, and also to look deep inside ourselves to the place of inner knowing.

Our chart may be able to suggest a meaning in events that helps us to accept them, it may offer a direction to look, and help us to recognise that the voice we hear is truly our own guidance, but it is not appropriate to use astrology to make our decisions for us, nor to tell us what is the truth. Astrology itself can never give us the answers.

Chapter 1
Overviews

The Centre of the Circle

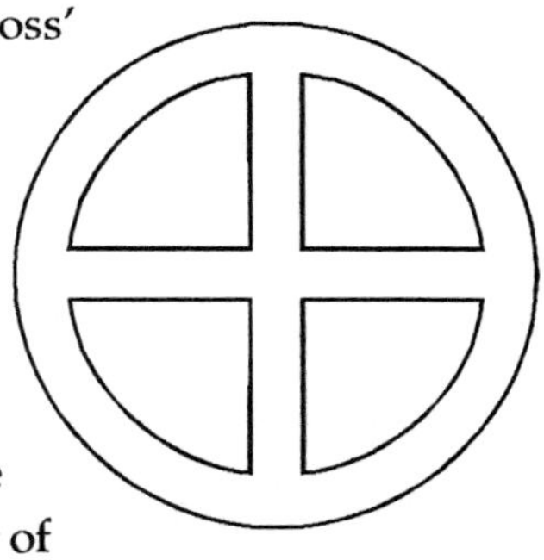

The symbol of the 'circle and cross' is often used to represent healing: the unity of the circle and the harmony of the four equal arms represent the principle of total health on all levels.

We begin with a circle to represent all there is, all there can be, all potential, out of time. A point in the centre of the circle symbolises the point of creation where time begins, potential starts to become actual and there is separation. In astrology, the circle with a dot in the middle represents the Sun, the great light that hides the source of all life, the Sun itself being the creative source of light and life on Earth. If we extend the dot in the circle so that it becomes the two lines that divide the circle in half both vertically and horizontally, it gives us four equal quarters, and a cross of four equal arms, the astrological symbol for the Earth.

The dot is where the two lines cross and, when the four elements of manifested material life are balanced, that dot will be in the centre of the circle. It is that centre point that links us with the timelessness of Unity: when we are balanced in ourselves, the Source is accessible to us, transforming our earthly experience with understanding and joy. To develop a powerful, effective, and happy state, we need to contact that centre of our being and there we can be in touch with our own innate wisdom and the essence of all life.

Astrology has the potential to help us reach that centre point in ourselves. If we let the circle represent all astrological potential, we can divide it horizontally and vertically to find the centre. Astrology can be divided into a science and an art, and also divided into its general use and personal use. Firstly we will divide the circle horizontally, one half illustrating its use at a general level, showing our *similarities* as human beings, and the other half showing its application on a personal level. At the personal level, individual birth charts are the tools which show our *differences* from each other.

We are the same only different - Astrology as general and as personal

There are many books and workshops to help us 'unpeel the onion' of our personality to reach the centre. Because they are structured for many people at the same time, they are generalised and based on our similarities. We are the same in that we are all human, we have parents, we grow through childhood and adolescence, and are subject to family and social conditioning. Everyone has a personality with many facets and we share feelings with the same names such as guilt, anger, pleasure. Everyone also has the possibility of reaching that point within themselves which feels like the truth of their centre. Much of what is written and spoken addresses these similarities, with ideas such as taking responsibility for one's life, accepting people as they are, thinking positively to create positive experience, meditating to make contact with one's centre. We all need these teachings, and working with others, all using the same method, helps to give us a sense of our 'oneness' with each other

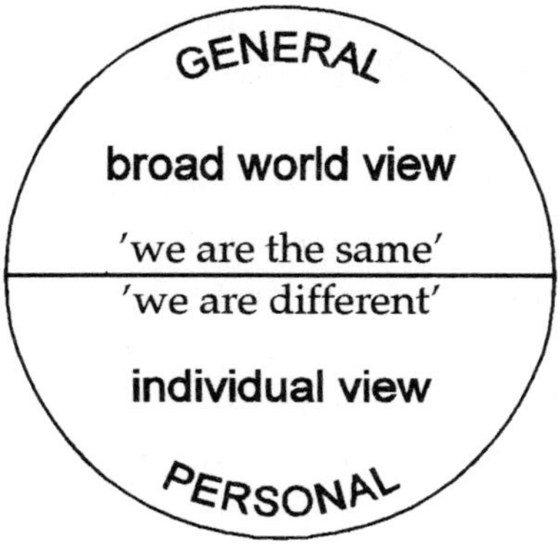

However, at a personality level, which is where we mostly live, we are very different from each other and the methods of working with our own personal unfolding need to be as individual as we are ourselves. Every now and then in life a person who is working towards a new, more aware, style of life will need individual help, as they reach an unconscious attitude block or a repetitive behavioural plateau where the general words cannot be assimilated and used. They may work with a therapist of some kind or a friend, or may choose to work alone but, without some sort of map as an unbiased overview, an individual can get lost. Astrology is a system, as ancient as humanity, which offers each individual a personal map. This map, or chart, is created mathematically from scientifically derived information based on the individual's time and place of birth. All this is as unbiased as one's reflection in a flat glass. No judgement is offered by the chart, simply a statement of how it is.

The branch of astrology that fascinates most people is natal astrology, that supremely personal view showing the reflection of *your* life on earth, and *your* individual character, different from any other. Your birth chart reflects your personality with all its individuality and potential. It also shows the tendencies that follow unconscious use, and which may keep that potential from unfolding as far as it could.

The interpretation of astrology that is not so often considered is the broader view, where we use the Zodiac Signs, the celestial bodies, and the twelve divisions of the sky to describe the human condition in a *general* sense. Confusion can arise through the use of general astrology in magazine pages which is often written in more individualistic terms than is appropriate. This is a legitimate use of planets in Zodiac Signs, but can be misleading when it is taken too personally.

The general view describes the whole of humanity, each person described by the combination of all the Signs, and containing all the planetary principles. The most complete reflection of humanity as a whole, and even of one individual person, is the entire sky. If we want to see a reflection of our individual self, we have only to look at the night sky with all its wonders. Even then, all that we can see on a clear night far from city lights, is only half of our reflection, the other half being beneath the earth.

It is good to remember that we help ourselves evolve not only by learning to accept our particular reflection in our birth charts, and learning to understand how it is for other people shown in theirs. It *is* all this, but it is also recognizing how we are all little splinters of the great human hologram, described in the Zodiac Story (Chapter 2). Each one of us contains the whole human experience, and also each of us is individually expressed by the whole: that is to say, 'I AM all of it', and also 'it all reflects me'.

We are all human beings, different because of our different perceptions of life; and also each one of us, as part of Oneness, is a doorway for the expression of all creation. Bearing this in mind, we recognise the need to balance the two halves of the circle and align ourselves with the line across the centre.

Logic and Intuition - the Science and the Art of Astrology

We can also divide the astrological circle vertically, the scientific method on the left, and the art of practice on the right.

The science of astrology takes the movements of stars and planets, from the point of view of the Earth, drawn as a two-dimensional pattern, and describes it using the principles and meanings laid down over centuries of experience. In natal astrology this drawing is a chart or picture of the time and place of birth of a character, and the description is a character analysis which can be run off a computer. If the information built into the program is accurate and well expressed, a printout for a particular birth time will be a good analysis.

The art of astrology is the intuitive blending, or synthesis, of the astrological principles involved in a chart, in order to interpret that chart to its owner in a helpful and appropriate way. Even people with almost identical charts would receive individual readings relevant to their experiences, and addressing the roots of their beliefs about life. This kind of chart reading involves an intuitive rapport with the person in order to describe the chart in a way they recognise as themselves.

A person will feel such a chart reading as confirming their experience of themselves and their life. It will show them how it is possible to create more enjoyable experiences at work, in relationships, and so on. It will give them a more conscious sense of their own potential as actually achievable, and a feeling that they are valuable people worthy of self-acceptance. A good reading will enable a person to align with their most satisfying course of action, and will suggest what would feel good to focus on next.

The science of astrology requires use of the left brain, while the art is an expression of the right brain. Without the art of astrology, one can be an expert in the science of astrology yet give a useless, even damaging, interpretation of a birth chart. On the other hand, without an accurate chart, even practising the art in a healing way will still give false information. What is needed is a balance between the two sides to align ourselves with the line down the centre.

Astrology as a guide to the centre point

In a reading, we need to help a person balance the way they see themselves, both as an individual (their differences), and as someone in relationship with the rest of humanity (their similarities with others), so that their personal development will not cut them off from society. This balancing also allows each individual's growth and greater awareness to 'salt the pot' of humanity, because every individual development, however apparently small, is reflected in the whole.

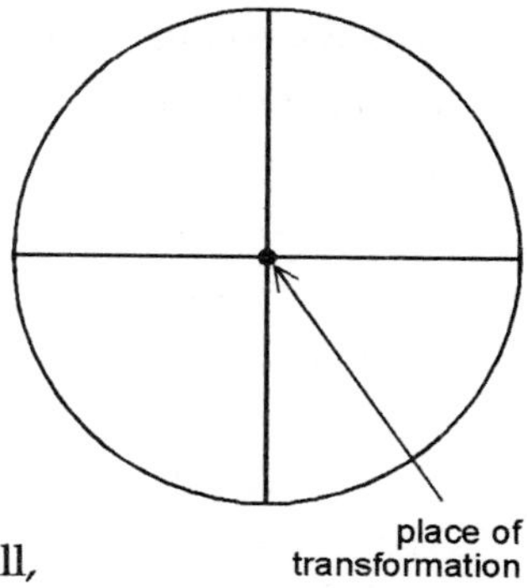

In each of the following chapters this first division of the circle will be made by talking about the general meaning of the astrological principles in a first section headed '*Ways in which we are the same*', followed by a second section headed '*Ways in which we are different*' containing the particular, individual use of these principles for personal understanding, relationship and growth.

When we use scientifically calculated and drawn birthcharts and the ancient principles of astrology, and practise the interpretation of them as an art, we strengthen the link between the two hemispheres of the brain. This second division of the circle will be made clear by the words themselves speaking sequentially to the left brain, and the symbols and many of the ideas speaking to the right brain. Shifting ideas from left brain words to right brain understanding, and back, will also be facilitated by carrying out the exercises given from time to time throughout this book.

To be on both dividing lines at once, puts us on the dot in the centre of the circle, the hole in the middle where we can fall through the centre of our being into All That Is. Enabling a person to get to that place in themselves allows a transformative experience to occur in a chart reading. When we read a chart well, we are combining the intellectual and intuitive faculties of the brain and expressing them through our heart.

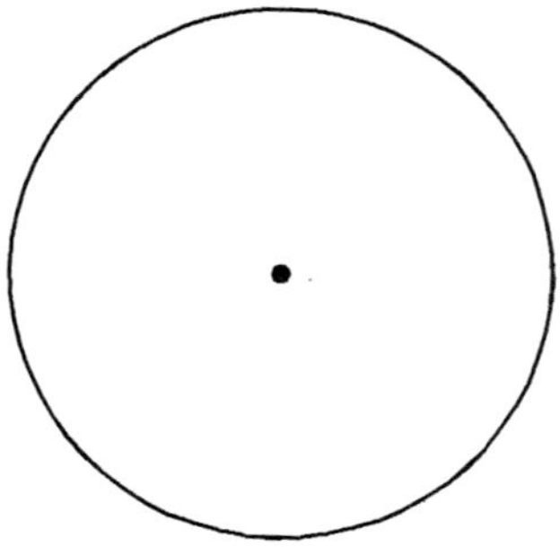

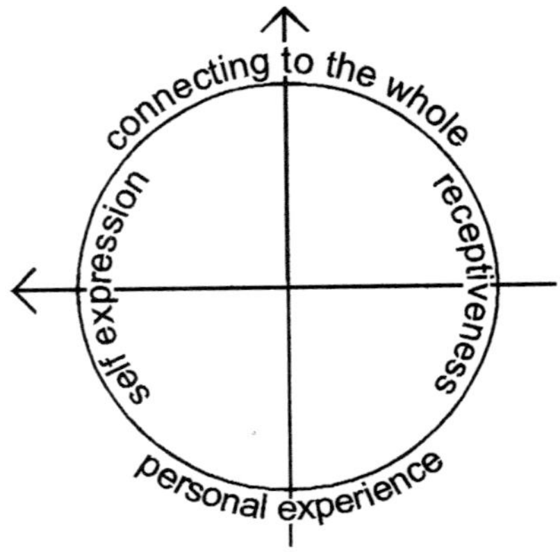

From the spirit symbol of the Sun, the dot within the circle, we have arrived at the Earth symbol, the circle and cross, which is the shape of the astrological birth chart itself. The chart shows how we balance our personal experience (below the horizon) with our connection to the whole (above the horizon), and our self-expression (left side) with our receptiveness (right side). All this is contained within the circle of Zodiac Signs and Houses which express all potential human experience.

Astrology in a nutshell

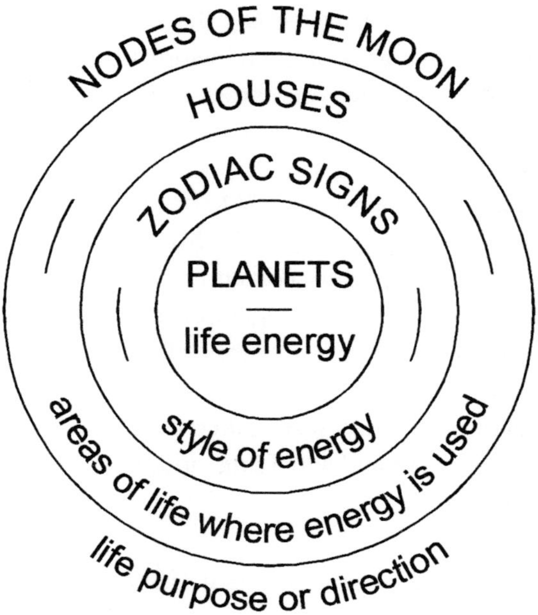

An **astrological birthchart** consists of:

1 the **<u>planets</u>** representing **life energy** flowing through us with different functions,

2 in **<u>Zodiac Signs</u>** showing the **style or manner** in which each energy is expressed,

3 in **<u>Houses</u>** showing which **areas of our life** encourage us to use that energy, and which activities get the energy going.

4 The planets are said to be in relationship with each other when the number of degrees between them is significant. **<u>Aspects</u>** is the name given to planetary

relationships, each specific number of degrees indicating a different reaction between them. I generally use only numbers which are multiples of thirty degrees, thereby keeping the scientific side simple. There are six of them including the conjunction, and each one shows a different relationship between the two planets.

5 Basically, this is all that needs to be known about, but I like to include **the Nodes of the Moon** which suggest the most satisfying direction and how to achieve it. I use this axis because finding a direction or possible purpose for this life can integrate all the other factors in the chart, and thus help the person to integrate their divergent personality traits. It creates a life 'story' which feels right and satisfying, and helps the person accept themself.

It is crucial to remember that astrology neither makes us what we are, nor creates our life. The birth chart describes us, as a map describes a landscape or a mirror reflects a face. Our personality is our spirit's choice, and what we do in our life is up to us.

Transformative chart reading

We need to be gentle, accepting and loving to anyone whose birth chart we read, including ourselves. It is not easy to understand our own chart because we have so much assumed 'knowledge' of ourselves, so, if we begin by imagining our unknown self sitting beside us, it will be easier to create an attitude of really wanting to know this self better.

For the purpose of looking at a birthchart usefully, we need to work within two beliefs: firstly, that each person's life can be meaningful to them; and secondly, that experience is useful when one learns something positive from it. The added sense that life of itself is a joy, combined with a love of people as individuals, will make your time together a healing experience for the recipient, regardless of how much or little astrological knowledge you have. It helps the person to be open to change and growth during the reading.

One of the most valuable results of a chart reading is the ability it gives us to detach a little from our personality, enabling us to see ourselves. At the beginning of a reading, there may be some time spent talking about the planets in Signs at a light level so that the person can start to look at themselves in this detached way, even seeing whereabouts on the chart their characteristics are reflected.

Then we will need to focus on the places where they are having trouble in life, giving away their power to situations or other people. These painful areas will be shown by planetary principles that are in an uncomfortable position in the chart, and the person is likely to want to reject those experiences. As the whole chart is always in operation, the rejected energies do not disappear, but will be reflected by the behaviour of relatives, colleagues and bosses, and difficulties will show up in relationship with those people. So we describe the characteristic that is being projected out onto others.

It is a good idea, when searching for a way of describing a particular planet in a chart, first to give the person an idea of what it might feel like, and then have them describe in their own words how it feels to them and what actually seems to happen in that area of life. We might also ask them why they feel the need or desire to judge and reject a particular feeling or behaviour, to discover what their difficulty is with handling that energy themselves. Individuals are far more complex than the few celestial details we put in a chart, and an astrologer can learn something new with every reading.

At this point in a reading, depending on one's abilities in counselling, it may be relevant to speak of the early life where the difficulties appeared to begin. It is best to avoid *blaming* parents because this perpetuates a sense of being a victim. So together we might even create images of possible past lives where earlier experiences could have happened that have been replaying in this life because of our traumatised expectation. It is not important to be 'accurate' about past lives. The crucial factor is whether it 'feels right' to the recipient.

Using past lives as a description of origins of reaction and behaviour is useful in that it takes the fear we have of people and events away from the future, and places it in the past in a time that was very different from this life. The feared event has already happened and what one has now is only the memory of the trauma. It may be that the person we have been reacting to recently merely reminds us of someone we tangled with painfully in the past.

Once we realise that it is our fear and expectation of remembered events that has been recreating our experiences we are free to let go of the expectation; and understanding that our reactions probably had a very good cause, we can accept our pain with more kindness.

Using our knowledge of astrological meanings, however small we feel it to be, we can, at this point, show what the rejected energy could be like when expressed in more positive ways, what ability it might show. As the recipient accepts the energy in that form, they begin to feel it in themselves. They find both, that this energy feels natural to them, and also that the ability that goes with it is something they already do in certain circumstances with positive results.

As the person integrates the idea of these characteristics, it becomes possible for us to describe their potential, shown by the rest of the chart, in terms that they feel is actually possible to achieve. The order of the reading does not have to be as stated here. The best guides are the way the conversation goes with the recipient, and one's own intuition. Many negatively experienced issues may arise during this reading, requiring positive and useful vision to balance them. The truth is that every ability needs care when used, and every difficulty teaches a skill. If we cannot find the balancing vision, trusting that it exists will be enough to keep us steady.

In the following chapters the Zodiac Signs, planets and Houses are expressed in ways that will give the reader the sense of a complete picture, enabling chart readings to be transformative experiences.

The recipient of such a reading will be unfolding inside while the reading proceeds; during the process, changes will be occurring in their mental structuring, and their programmed beliefs and expectations. Because of these developments, changes will also be occurring in the emotions. Sometimes the person will shift position suddenly, sigh deeply, cry or laugh, all showing an internal shift. Through these emotional and bodily changes, the hormones, the glands that secrete them, and the whole energy system of the body, is undergoing a shake-up, a healing.

This ultimately affects the basic life programming in the genes and DNA because the physical body is structured according to the energy system. The person is brought into the present time at a very deep level through the acceptance of who they really are - the transformation. It can be likened to developmental homoeopathy; the potency of the remedy in a transformative chart reading is the vibrational sound of the spoken word accurately prescribed.

As the genes are affected, what was hereditary is changed for future generations. It is not necessary to pass on to one's children everything that has come down from the ancestors. Changing the structure of bodies being born, through releasing restrictive belief patterns, enables finer, wiser spirits to incarnate without getting lost in the negative programming of our present world. We need them!

Chapter 2
The Zodiac

Part 1
Ways in which we are the same

The system of Four Elements - how they make the twelve Zodiac Signs

The system of Four Elements is an ancient way of describing 'all that is'. The idea states that that everything is composed of a combination of four 'elements': Earth and Water, Air and Fire, like the building blocks of DNA. There is a chant:

"Earth is my body, Water, my blood,
Air is my breath, and Fire, my spirit."

Added together, the four elements create 'ether' or life force. Their perfect balance in an individual person shows as physical, emotional and mental health, combined with personal spiritual contact.

Each element has three qualities, or ways of being. Cardinal is pushing outward, Fixed is within itself, and Mutable is changeable.

An element in its **Cardinal** state
expresses towards the world.
An element in its **Fixed** state
is in its own being.
An element in its **Mutable** state
adapts to circumstance and pressure.

Imagine each of the four elements drawn as a triangle with its three points as the qualities of Cardinal, Fixed and Mutable. Evenly placed in a circle, these four triangles make twelve points on the circumference, which link in with the twelve Zodiac Signs.

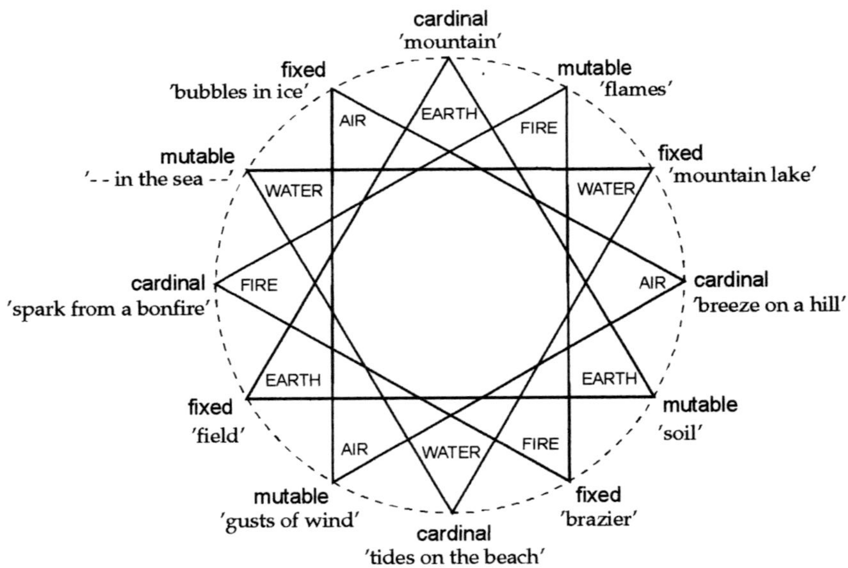

<u>Each element has a meaning</u> in terms of personality traits, and in the following table, words are grouped to aim towards those meanings. Each quality, each of the three ways of being an element, has been given an image in this table, to assist the intuitive, conceptual side of the brain to

join in the quest for understanding. Those images are expanded in 'The Zodiac Story' further through this chapter. Eventually, through allowing all the symbols to trigger understanding, each Zodiac symbol will become a key to the door of one of the twelve Signs. Open the door with that key and your intuition can enter into one twelfth of All That Is.

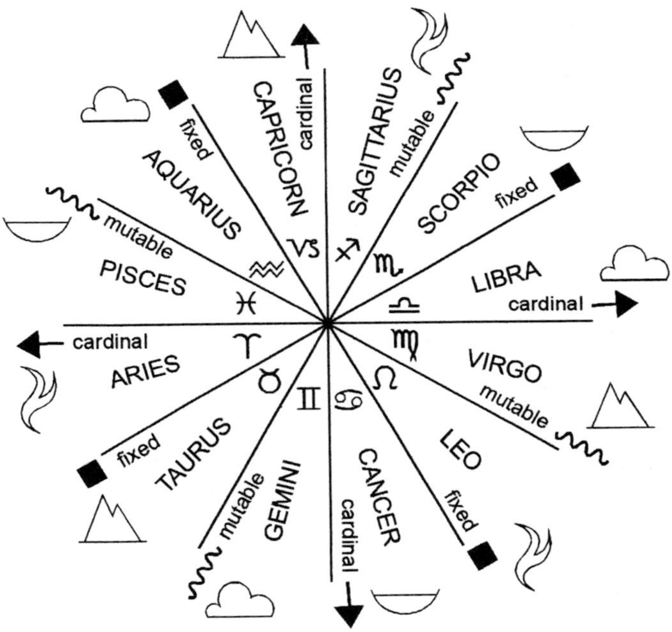

FIRE - the realm of transformation. It can be enthusiastic, loving, affectionate, warm. It can also be fanatical or idealistic, destructive or creative with life energy, anger and passion, and it always needs fuel.

Cardinal	**Aries**	"spark from a bonfire"
Fixed	**Leo**	"brazier"
Mutable	**Sagittarius**	"flames"

AIR - the realm of thought and ideas. It has clarity, fast movement, speech, logic, elegance. Sometimes it can be cold and unfeeling, using logic against common sense, and it needs freedom.

Cardinal	**Libra**	"breeze on a hill"
Fixed	**Aquarius**	"bubbles in ice"
Mutable	**Gemini**	"gusts of wind"

WATER - the realm of emotion and psychic experience. It is irrational, cleansing, flowing, sensitive, gentle, the nurturing womb. It can be overwhelming, pressuring or flooding, and it needs movement.

Cardinal	**Cancer**	"tides on the beach"
Fixed	**Scorpio**	"mountain lake"
Mutable	**Pisces**	". . . in the sea . . ."

EARTH - the realm of material effect. It is practical, heavy, slow, sensible, serious, supportive, nourishing. It can be stuck, rigid, depressed, and it needs time.

Cardinal	**Capricorn**	"mountain"
Fixed	**Taurus**	"field"
Mutable	**Virgo**	"soil"

Exercises:

1 Meditate on each element as a group of three images, noticing how they differ.

2 Choose other images to express the different qualities of each element.

The Zodiac Signs as twelve pieces of a whole process

Just for a moment, see each activity you do as the process of cutting a round cake. Choose a place to begin and cut the cake into twelve slices. The beginning of cutting the first slice needs the courage to take a step where no-one else has been before. Aries is about beginnings: it is open, fresh, ready to start something new, full of energy, impatient to see results. The other eleven slices will be cut in order round the cake until the twelfth, which, like Pisces, completes the 'disintegration' of the whole cake into parts.

Each of the twelve Signs in the Zodiac has a specific meaning which relates to its place in the process, from Aries at the beginning to Pisces, the twelfth and last.

You could have cut the cake into a different number of slices, say thirteen or ten, but each slice would then be a different size: that is to say, the meaning of each piece in terms of its part in the process, would be a bit different. If you divide anything into pieces, then every piece is needed to make the thing whole.

The Seasons as a Cycle

The traditional image of the natural seasons in England can be used as an example of the cycle of the Zodiac. This is because the qualities of each season match those of the Signs containing the Sun at that time of year. The cycle is divided into four: Spring, Summer, Autumn and Winter, each with its Cardinal Sign stating its beginning, its Fixed Sign sure of the season's identity in the middle, and its Mutable Sign as it begins to transform into the following season.

♈ 1 **Aries - Cardinal Spring,** the energy bursting out of the ground as though impatient after being confined by the cold; new plans for the year. Starts at the Equinox, about 21st March. ↑

♉ 2 **Taurus - Fixed Spring,** we become used to the sense of growth, fresh new green everywhere, the May pole comes out, the bull reminds us of fertility rites. ■

♊ 3 **Gemini - Mutable Spring,** the gusty winds are friendly and promise warmth not yet to be trusted, preparing for the Summer. ∿

♋ 4 **Cancer - Cardinal Summer,** the Summer Solstice, 21st June, it is the time of rising energy, of maximum growth, the Earth nurturing all her children. ↑

♌ 5 **Leo - Fixed Summer,** we have come to expect hot days, the leaves have been around long enough to be dusty, children are on holiday from school hopefully having fun. ■

♍ 6 **Virgo - Mutable Summer**, the leaves are starting to change colour and we notice the shortening days; we have the sense that the fruits will not be there for ever, and begin the labour of the harvest. ∿

♎ 7 **Libra - Cardinal Autumn**, having gratefully harvested the fruits of our labour, at the Equinox (23rd September) we give, to balance what we have been given. ↑

♏ 8 **Scorpio - Fixed Autumn**, it becomes clear that we must get ready for the coming cold, preparing to protect ourselves; chill and damp; Hallowe'en and fireworks round the bonfire in the dark. ■

♐ 9 **Sagittarius - Mutable Autumn**, we have our warmer clothes on now, preparing for Christmas; lights, and longer evenings collect us round the fire to pass the time. ∿

♑ 10 **Capricorn - Cardinal Winter,** the Winter Solstice, 21st December, marks the power underground, the plentiful food and gifts at Christmas supplied by one who has either worked for it, or who has it by inheritance. ↑

♒ 11 **Aquarius - Fixed Winter,** the cold has set in, ice and snow and the ground so hard that nothing can get through except the snowdrop, a vision of perfect purity. ■

♓ 12 **Pisces - Mutable Winter**, the ice begins to melt, more flowers push through, but the cold keeps returning, change is in the air but uncertain, and who knows what the next year will bring? ∿

Seasons are different in every country, but the cycle of beginning, growth, maturing, digesting, dispersion and new beginning is the cycle of life itself. If any one piece of this process is left out, the rest of the process cannot happen.

The Zodiac Signs as twelve pieces of a whole personality

As it is with the Zodiac as a whole process, so it is when the Zodiac is used to describe the personality: if any Sign is removed, the personality will not be complete. We each need to have the qualities of every Zodiac Sign in order to be a whole person.

If we all need to have every Zodiac Sign in our personality somewhere, it is very important to be able to see the best side of each Sign as well as its problems. Sometimes people talk about one Sign or another as though life would be better without it, but this would just make life incomplete. If we can learn to use the best of each Sign, we will be honest, useful and happy, fully rounded people. Also, we will be able to understand other people much better and recognise what is valuable in them, no matter what Sign they are.

Learning to express love through each of the twelve Signs is a way to become aware of our Godself, the highest expression of our centre. It is like the twelve disciples together in spirit reflect Jesus, or twelve consecutive semitones on a piano in sound span an octave: each one of the twelve is an individual expression of one part of the essence, which has twelve aspects.

There follows a list of all the Zodiac Signs, and the pieces of your personality they reflect. Some of them will be familiar - pieces you know that you have. Others might be pieces you admire in other people, and there may be one or two that you have never thought about.

The (bracketed) words are picture images that express some of the essence of the Sign. The underlined word is a quality of each Sign that would help us to enjoy life and be valuable people. The *italic* words suggest a focus that assists in developing the underlined quality.

Under each Sign there are also listed some activities in which the abilities of the Sign would be useful, although most of our activities do need the abilities of more than one Sign.

♈ **Aries** (spark from a bonfire) courageous for new beginnings, fresh, ready to start something new, full of energy, impatient to see results, ready to attack rather than be frustrated or stuck, can be aggressive.
Useful when starting something new, and also when being self-motivated.
Learning to use the right amount of energy for each situation.

♉ **Taurus** (field) grounded, dependable, practical, earthy, helping people to be healthy by sharing earth energy, slow, quiet, concerned about security, can be stubborn and unchanging.
Useful in gardening, cooking etc. and when others need steady support.
Learning to make peaceful contact with nature.

♊ **Gemini** (gusts of wind) able to talk with anyone, finding out things and telling people, imagining or working it out, at least two of everything, sometimes charming - sometimes silent, changing between two personalities, two homes, two jobs, can be unreliable.
Useful when needing information, putting people at ease, writing.
Learning to use both sides of your brain - balancing intuition and logic .

♋ **Cancer** (tides on the beach) emotionally sensitive, up and down moods, family-loving, half childish and half like a loving parent, caring or needing to be cared for, nurturing, can hold on to people too hard.
Useful when home-making, empathising with a friend, giving quality time to little children.
Learning to be steady and supportive in emotional situations.

♌ **Leo** (brazier) open hearted, loving, dramatic, encouraging, enjoy leading or entertaining other people, proud of one's self, sunny, can be too loud and pushy, pride can be easily hurt.
Useful at parties, when others are feeling down, giving a talk or teaching.
Learning to stay loving and positive no matter what other people think.

♍ **Virgo** (soil) making things better, helpful, aiming for perfection, efficient, wanting to be right, can be critical, self-critical or fussy.
Useful when putting things in order, being careful making things, sorting out what is important.
Learning to accept things and people as they are, as a basis for improving life.

♎ **Libra** (breeze on a hill) diplomatic, relating pleasantly, balancing your interest in *you* with your interest in other people, peace-making, supporting the under-dog, listening to all sides in an argument, can be hesitant for fear of spoiling things.
Useful in meetings, choosing colours, clothes or decor.
Learning to gather all the information necessary to realise the correct decision.

♏ **Scorpio** (mountain lake) emotional understanding, feeling things very deeply, strong, knowing about the difficult side of life, wanting to know what is going on under the surface, intense, can be unkind and want revenge.

Useful when you need to be determined, for understanding and helping deep hurt in others.

Learning to use painful times for growth and understanding.

♐ **Sagittarius** (flames) enthusiastic, optimistic - always seeing the positive possibilities, interested in everything, full of fun, enjoying discussion about life, travelling, teaching, exploring, can be rushing about or failing to explain what you mean clearly.

Useful when enthusiasm is needed.

Learning to share your interests, so that other people can expand their thinking.

♑ **Capricorn** (mountain) working to get what you want, doing your best, careful, results more important than feelings, strong and reliable, sometimes takes too much responsibility, can be too serious or bossy.

Useful for organising other people, when working out how to do something practical.

Learning to reach what you decide you want, by using intention rather than heavy labour.

♒ **Aquarius** (bubbles in ice) having an over-view, seeing the best way to organise everybody, knowing the best way to do things, wanting equal opportunities for everyone, feeling free, observing people, can seem cold and unfriendly.

Useful when others panic, when on your own.

Learning that everyone has something to give, and that although people are equal in value they are not all the same.

♓ **Pisces** (. . . in the sea. . .) putting other people first, knowing that you are really a light spirit in an earthly body, very emotional, feeling everybody's feelings, wanting to help everybody feel better, sometimes feeling resentful, forgetting to ask for help.

Useful when meditating, in counselling.

Learning to be in touch with spirit joy, so that it can be shared with everyone you meet.

Exercises:

1 All activities need one or more Signs - think of other things that you do, and ponder on which Signs you need to do them well.

2 If you know your chart, see if you have any planetary energy in these Signs.

3 Whether you know this or not, try to act these Signs to the best of your ability when actually engaged in the activity

The Zodiac Story

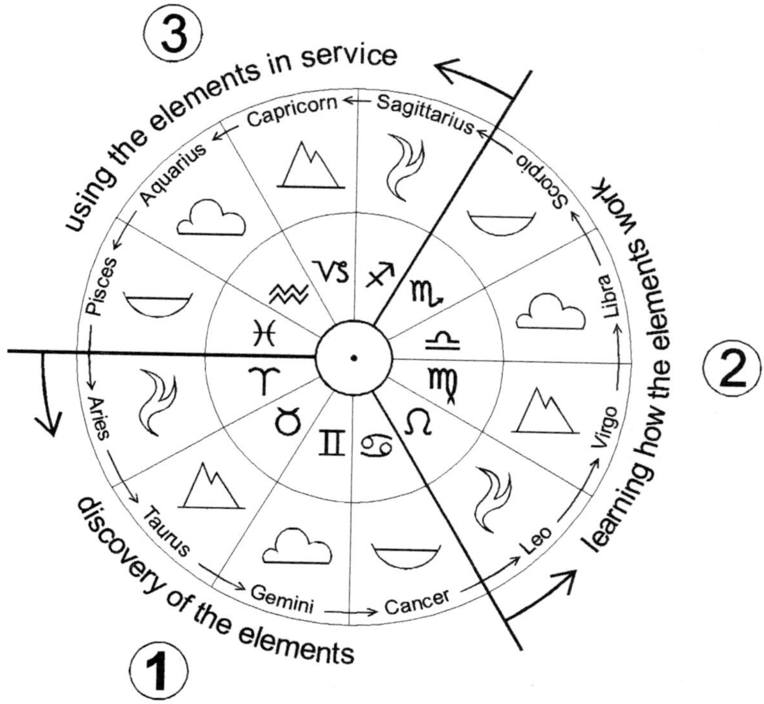

The meaning of the Zodiac is inherent in creation because it describes any cyclic process. I like describing the Zodiac as the process of a spirit evolving a clear and complete human character through experience in Earth. It is our own story. Each Sign can be said to represent a stage of life, a quality of experience, a way of feeling in relation to the world; and each one of us experiences all the Signs as we go through our life.

Let us imagine, insofar as we are able, the all-inclusive Oneness becoming the Source of all life, which proceeds to extend its divine fire. The extensions feel individual (Aries) and make the original error of thinking they are separate from their Source. These individual sparks, or spirits, manifest surroundings (Taurus) to push against in order to become aware, understanding and effective in the same way as their creator. The surroundings are earth, the focus of experience, and the Zodiac describes that experience as twelve lessons expressing growth. In this story, the perfect growth of the spirit through one round of the Zodiac Signs creates the perfect human archetype through which the spirit becomes aware again of its Oneness with the Source (Pisces).

The movement through the Signs can be seen as breathing. The out-breaths are in Fire and Air; the in-breaths are in Earth and Water. This makes the pattern of out - Fire, in - Earth, out - Air, in - Water, repeated twice more, making six great breaths in all. Now let us tell the story of this great life development:

♈ Aries "spark from a bonfire"

a spark of life, tiny but hugely bright, brave, with no thought for the future, catching the eye for a moment, inspiring hope

At first there was only the sea of unified unconsciousness and, in a moment, one drop of that ocean used its energy to leap out of the waves into free space. This is the experience of Aries, this first thought that, as there is self, then the rest of existence is separate. The energy is powerful and drives the spirit forward into discovering what this "self" is like.

In the Aries character you find a wonder about life, an ability to be amazed as though this is their first view of the world. The drive to discovery can sometimes knock other people flat with its naive exuberance.

Aries is often experienced by others as aggressive and combative, certainly competitive, but this can be due to the vague fear of disappearing back into the oblivion they experience as Pisces. The competition is to discover the limits of the newly found self, rather than to have power over another. The combativeness in the face of perceived blocks is an expression of frustration of that energy which always drives the character onwards.

If weapons are taken up against an Aries, it is found that the confidence is often only apparent, not real, and what appears to be selfishness is due to thoughtlessness and a lack of understanding of other people's needs. All can be remedied with explanation and discussion - after all, Aries rules the head: the ventricles of the brain are shaped like rams' horns, the ram being the Aries symbol.

In Aries the spirit learns to let raw energy flow through, giving life to their own and other people's ideas, starting projects and always moving on to new realms. It is the discovery of Fire, the element that represents energy and expresses itself through activity, humour and affection. Later, in Leo, the second Fire Sign, controlling Fire has priority, and in Sagittarius, the third and last Fire Sign, Fire needs to be used constructively.

♉ **Taurus** *"field"*

a field, secure delicious pasture,
meadow flowers in the sun,
breathing sweet and lazy warmth

Having developed consciousness of individuality and an energetic drive, the spirit is ready to gather a physical manifestation round itself. The Sign of Taurus is the first contact with Earth, and the earth force flows freely through a Taurus character, spreading a relaxing atmosphere towards whoever is around. For this reason Taurus is the natural physical healer of the Zodiac, needing only to contact another person with their hands in a pat on the back or a brief cuddle to create a sense of harmony and physical well-being in the other. At its most powerful, that touch can remove blockages in a person's energy flow and heal their body.

The Earth element represents the material world, and expresses itself through stability, solidity and dependability. The symbol of Taurus is the bull. We most often think of a bull in its own field, perhaps with the odd cow around for his natural gratification. It is as though he owns his patch, and the world can do as it likes outside the fence.

His anger is aroused only by the trespasser or anyone who attempts to take what Taurus regards as his own, and it stops again as his furious charge reaches his own boundary and his possessions are returned.

It is the fertility of the bull that indicates Taurus, its slowness to begin movement, its contentment with enough worldly pleasures. In the Taurus character this can look like a stubborn, stick-in-the-mud attitude or laziness, but there is a fear of insecurity, not knowing what is going on outside the fence or how one will survive if things change. When

Taurus is in any way upset or suffering, contact with nature will heal them.

The spirit in Taurus is learning about the flow of Earth energy, the limits of the body and its energy, and the extent of physical needs. In the second Earth Sign, Virgo, the lesson is how the material world works, and in Capricorn, the third and last Earth Sign, the knowledge is applied for the benefit of the world at large.

♊ **Gemini** *"gusts of wind"*

gusts of wind whirling flashes of news around and letting go to play with leaves, dancing with us and then gone

With consciousness of itself and the ability to gather a physical form, the spirit is now ready to explore mentally everything that it sees as not itself, through Gemini. This is the spirit's first contact with Air, the element that represents the world of ideas. It expresses itself through thought and the communication of that thought. The Gemini mind goes out looking for ideas and things, to understand them sufficiently to name them, and then to communicate that understanding to others.

It is not necessary for the Gemini character to understand deeply, or to study a subject for a long time. The speedy grasp of essentials is all that is required to pass on the information, and then move on to something else. It is not even necessary that the information should add up to make a larger picture; that will be the task in Sagittarius. For Gemini such adding together would take time they would rather spend finding more bits. This can look like a butterfly mind, always touching ideas but never going deep enough to see where they lead. But the communication of these ideas to the public is invaluable, and the Gemini character has already developed the ability to communicate with anyone. Their interest, combined with flexibility of expression, gives them the knack of charming all kinds of people into conversation and the versatility of their mind is well suited to learning anybody's language. On the other hand, the need to communicate can lead to empty chatter that is difficult to stop.

The symbol of Gemini is the twins, a symbol of duality, perhaps the two sides of the brain: left hemisphere having the ability to think logically, and make words and sentences; the right hemisphere housing the ability to understand at a glance, to intuit, to imagine. There is often found in Gemini behaviour, two characters within one person, one outward and communicative, the other a mystery, sometimes silent, even depressed or morose.

Perhaps the secret of this dual personality rests in the blending of the two hemispheres, and the communication that is needed may be between the two halves of the brain. The silent half may need to communicate the imaginative side through creativity without words. Whatever the solution, it can be witnessed that a Gemini person usually prefers to have at least two of everything, maybe to express their own inner differences.

The spirit in Gemini is flexing its mental muscles in order to build a clever and versatile brain, capable of questing far into the universe along logically constructed bridges, a truly wonderful tool. In the second Air Sign, Libra, that tool is used to explore relationship between people, and in the third and last Air Sign, Aquarius, the vision thus acquired is applied to the organisation of society as a whole.

♋ Cancer *"tides on a beach"*

tide advancing slowly closer and closer, wets our feet saltily; ebbing away before coming closer again

At last the spirit is ready for its baptism in Water, the last of the four elements in this sequence. Water, as an element in astrology, represents the world of emotion, the psychic world. The symbol of Cancer is said negatively to represent the claws of a crab. Positively it shows the arms and breasts of the mother. Cancer is the Sign of mother and child, enfolded so closely that they dream as one and live emotionally blended. The relationship begins in the womb, and so we could say that the spirit in Cancer draws its earthly material into the form of a foetus surrounded by the waters of the chosen mother's womb.

The mother is chosen in the sense that each spirit requires the genes and upbringing that will create the personality to be worked with in the coming life. This personality will be a blend of some of those difficulties that have still to be smoothed out from previous Earthly encounters, together with the abilities that are necessary to achieve that smoothing out and move the spirit further along the road to fulfilment.

The element of Water expresses itself through feeling. Like water, the sea of emotion surrounds all of us all the time, and fills, as it were, the psychic space between us, enabling us to register the feelings of another. The Cancer character experiences this psychic sea of emotion as waves of contentment or sadness or resentment or hilarity, like moods over which there is no control. They come and go like waves on the beach, like the tides, high and low and high again. There is no sense of a need to control these moods. "If I am low today, tomorrow my mood may be high again, or if not tomorrow then the next day." A feeling of anger will be contained and lived with, but of course those living around the Cancer person will feel the anger fill the room. Likewise the hilarity is infectious, and the contentment is warming.

Cancer reaches out to people emotionally to care for, to nurture, to mother, and often to receive all those things from another. To feel and to give the security of mother-love is a strong need. With such a need, the Cancer person is emotionally dependent on the one who is fulfilling the other side of the bond, be they "child" or "mother". This is where the clinginess of the crab is seen, and it tells us that only half the person is awake.

The real need is for Cancer to mother their own inner child so that they don't present a vacuum, a neediness of love, to the world. One way to do this is to imagine the child as a separate form. Each time the feelings of neediness for another person come up, those feelings can then be looked at as belonging to this imaginary child. Then we know what to do to help the child feel better: we would naturally hold and love a child in such distress. So we love and cuddle the imaginary child, and the sense of neediness is forgotten and eventually healed. Taking this child everywhere we go, our inner neediness begins to trust the adult we have become, and there will be a time when that child disappears because it has been re-integrated into our adult self.

From the security this gives their personality, the Cancer person is then able to give the love freely to others, not holding onto them when nurturing is no longer necessary, able to let their children come and go without strings attached. Mothering the inner child requires an attitude of gentle acceptance of everything expressed without judging it to be good or bad. When we judge our inner child, we freeze our growth with fear of disapproval and rejection.

Any emotion that occurs in us may once have been an essential reaction to a survival issue. We needed to feel the way we did. The only judgement of any value is whether the emotion is appropriate to the moment we are feeling it now. If we say the emotion is wrong, we freeze inside. If we can say "In what situation was this emotion appropriate?" and allow ourselves not to be wrong about that, then we can look again at the present moment and see it more clearly as it is. In this way the inner child grows up gradually, and we become more able to relate to situations and people as they really are.

The spirit in Cancer learns that although the emotions change, swell and fade like the Moon in its phases or the tides on the beach, there is a stable centre which is not affected by the surrounding conditions. The Moon is a globe and only its appearance changes. The sea is a stable quantity of water, only the very edges of its shape move a little, shifting its emphasis in one direction or another in accordance with the Moon. Identifying with that stable centre requires a trust that the Great World Mother will nourish us if we participate in her work of loving and caring for humanity in all its growing phases.

In Cancer the spirit learns to relax in the process of changing and in the face of powerful emotions, secure in the knowledge that life itself is creative, and will always nurture us with its abundance. The second Water Sign, Scorpio, explores the emotional aspect of relationships with others, and tries different ways to protect their own vulnerability. Pisces, the third and last Water Sign, uses the accumulated sensitivity about feelings, to serve all people and try to make the world a better place.

Ω Leo *"brazier"*

warm in the chilly evening, roasting nuts to share; heat from inside attracts a cosy group, don't put it out!

The spirit now learns to stand clear of dependence on others, to identify itself as an individual in the same way as it did in Aries, but now it can begin to to use the Fire of that drive to affect its surroundings. This stage in growth can be likened to the little child who is old enough to sit and smile and wave its imperious directions to doting admirers. All that is needed is that the admirers know the child's desires and those desires are fulfilled - as long as the desires can be put across by the child in an effective way. The question is how to be effective.

Usually a radiant smile is enough, but sometimes it may be necessary to resort to shouts and even powerful use of emotional force. The Leo character becomes adept at handling whichever method works - unless the family are not admiring of the radiation at all. Then the child will learn that radiating is not effective in survival and the result is a person who retires and is quiet and sad. The shoulders may be rounded protecting the damaged heart centre of their body. There is no joy here.

We need to know that, when the spirit expresses itself through Leo, radiation is the only means of communication that it has. Learning how to wield it without blasting other people too hard is difficult. If that radiation is unacceptable there is a complete loss of confidence and a collapse of the ego's ability to stand up. When ridiculed or criticised, that powerful presence can be seen to be the paper-thin protection of a child in need of constant encouragement. Radiation requires an enormous amount of energy, and when the Leo is ill or recovering from a setback, they will often hide from even closest friends to lick their wounds in peace. It is as though they cannot bear to be with people unless they can radiate.

There is another difficulty that Leo experiences, which is that of receiving feedback from their "audience". Radiating is an outflow, and the more energy the person feels they must put in to keep the outflow going, the less they are able to feel the response of the person they are flowing towards. So they are very likely to overdo the outflow, talk too much, laugh too hard, forget to listen. But in spite of all this, who does not smile back at the warmth, tolerate the pressure, and enjoy the love and laughter in the true Leo humour? Only one who is wrapped up in their own problems and needs to "have their turn" - or another Leo perhaps!

The spirit in Leo is learning courage to be like the sun and radiate regardless of the likes or dislikes of the surrounding people, and also to radiate only what is appropriate for the life of those surroundings. It is necessary to have courage to wield the Fire that gives warmth, that gives life and love, but it must be blended with observation and sensitivity, in order not to burn those loved.

♍ **Virgo** "soil"

crumbling earthy potential growth, clay, potential pots for use; earth's voice in tiny insect sounds, busy

Let's imagine the child a little older now, old enough to crawl about, getting into all the cupboards and pulling things out; also old enough to walk and reach to things above head height, including pan handles on the stove. Curiosity motivates an exploration of the physical world - what is it like? how does it fit together? what is it made of? how much pressure will it take? The exploration is of a mental nature, questioning, examining, all with the ultimate view of improving things, sometimes creating quite a mess in the initial process!

The Virgo character is becoming adept at spotting the flaw and pointing it out so that it can be put right. However, most of the Zodiac Signs are fairly content to leave the material world as it is, and the perfecting Virgo is often accused of constant hair-splitting, nit-picking and criticism. Virgo-type people can feel as though they have a mission to tell the truth as they see it and thereby improve all things to maximum efficiency so that there is no waste. We could all do with a bit more of this characteristic for the sake of health and a balanced ecology, but it is exacting and often thankless work and the Virgo can easily feel over-burdened and misunderstood.

The worst of it is that their own actions and personality get inner criticism first. They are the ones that suffer most at their own hands. They can suffer from a constant inner nagging voice, correcting and complaining how they *never* get it right and *always* make mistakes because they feel they should be perfect. Other people's complaints simply confirm their view of their own imperfection.

The mistake that the Virgo character tends to make is to think that the perfection is something that can be achieved in the material world, that results should be perfect. They have an image of what perfection in a future situation will look like, but actually it is impossible to know what is perfectly appropriate until that moment in the future has become the present. The perfection we need to aim for is in the doing: it is possible for us to do our best, and that is perfect effort, moving with our sense of rightness as we go along. The results we get, no matter how we acted, perfectly serve to show us the style of our doing. So, as we grow, we can learn to improve our way of doing things. The necessary qualities of acute conscious focus and the ability to discriminate are part of the Virgo personality.

Sometimes Virgo people forget to take into account a person's emotional state, their level of maturity, even their present bodily limitations, and so their calculations as to what is possible for that person can be inaccurate. It is counter-productive to set standards for achievement that are not at present possible, because it is success that encourages; failure is not necessarily a spur to greater effort. Greater effort is not even necessarily the way to greater success. It may be relaxation that is missing, or a day off, or praise for the little that has so far been accomplished.

The spirit in Virgo is learning to understand the complex makeup of the world we live in and the laws by which it operates. The necessary coolness of the observation must not be allowed to cool either the heart's understanding of suffering or the value of play that was learned in Leo. With the previous lessons remembered, Virgo is the Sign of intelligent, helpful service to humanity on the material plane, the health and well-being of people, and the courage to speak the truth.

♎ **Libra** "breeze on a hill"

a questioning breeze blows steadily, bridging with a warming breath the distance between me and you

Now the child is a little older, perhaps at elementary school, making friends, learning how to relate to others, being very concerned about how other children think. Wearing what is acceptable and being liked are extremely important in this stage of growth.

The emphasis in Libra is again around understanding how things work and achieving perfection, but now it is in the realm of thought and communication with others (Air) instead of the material concerns of Earth-oriented Virgo. So Libra is concerned with relationships, discovering all the different ways of seeing a situation or person.

Many people think that because Libra is about balancing viewpoints, Librans should be making decisions. The way a Libran comes to a decision is to gather opinions, facts, attitudes, possibilities and probabilities and let all this add together in their mind. Eventually, when they can feel the wholeness of the situation, the correct decision will become obvious to them and they will act in accordance with the forces of the moment and create the most appropriate change.

The difficulties of indecision and hesitation come when a decision is called for too fast by someone who operates differently and doesn't understand the Libran process. Often people make the mistake of thinking that, because Librans *seem* so indecisive, they don't know their own minds, but in fact they are very clear, once the decision is made.

Another reason for the difficulty experienced by the

Libran character is a similar mistake to Virgo's, the belief that balance in relationships means being permanently pleasant. Balance consists of honesty and sweetness, night and day, dark and light, breathing in and breathing out, as long as we are alive on Earth. To have only day, or nothing but sweetness is not a state that applies to Earthly life. It denies the possibility of growth.

We grow through relationships which help us to see ourselves, to see our inappropriate habitual reactions and behaviour, and learn to shed them. Growth requires that out-of-date skins be shed, and it would be un-human not to hurt from time to time. So instead of regarding conflict and pain as failure, Librans need to realise that these are part of the process and, as long as they also help the other person to recover with love, all is well.

A common vision we have of a Libran is in discussion, hearing them put the opposite point of view to the one just expressed. It can lead to them being called argumentative, but it stems from the desire to have all views voiced. This will happen especially when they hear one person being over-praised, or run down. They need courage to stand apart from others in the group in order to promote a fair trial. The worst error in Libran terms is to have an opinion which is ill-informed. Better to have no final opinion at all.

The spirit in Libra is learning to balance dark with light, male with female, sensitivity with firmness, diplomacy with honesty, justice with mercy. It is learning to balance its personal needs with the good of all.

♏ Scorpio "mountain lake"

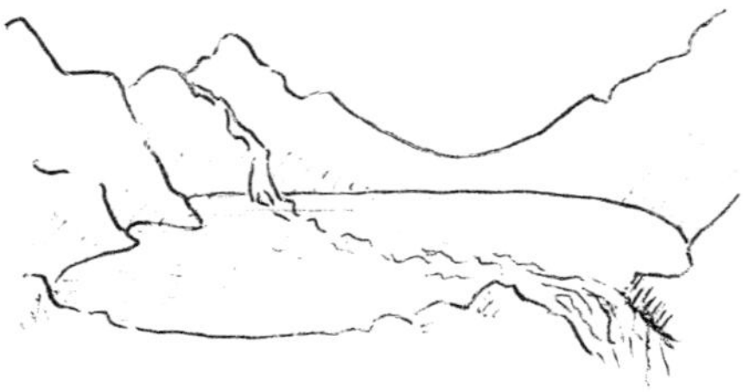

deep as the mountains are high, dark still surface; where a summit stream flows in, the water clears and overflows to feed the valley

The feeling of coming out of Libra into Scorpio is like the onset of adolescence, a plunging into the world of emotions. As puberty strikes, and male and female polarise energetically, the turbulent world of emotion is explored consciously for the first time, often through relationships where sexuality is veiled only loosely, if at all.

At last the feelings are fully admitted, where in Libra they were subdued for the sake of apparent peace. In Cancer, the first Water Sign, the emotions were stirred by the need for mother, comfort and nourishment. In Scorpio the need is for depth and emotional sharing in relationships. Feelings are so intense that the person can be very vulnerable to hurt. It is as though the Scorpio in us is where our capacity to experience emotions is being enlarged, like a container being ground out. The grinding is the painful part; the result of the grinding is the ability to contain a vast amount of emotion without spilling it all over the place as the other Signs do.

Imagine standing in the country watching the most glorious sunset of your life. A Scorpio character will be able to hold such an intense amount of joy that the concentration can bring union with the Source. The other Signs in the same situation will comment, cry, laugh, make a joke, suddenly remember what they meant to do this morning - anything rather than stay with the experience to completion.

What is more commonly noticed about Scorpio is that they hide their emotions behind their own particular smokescreen. Some will talk a lot about all sorts of things -

but not themselves. Some are silent as they observe others. Some are very caring of others but keep their own troubles quiet. Some keep the spotlight off themselves by stirring up the emotions of others. It is because they are more deeply vulnerable than we realise. Their most unhelpful form of protection from emotional hurt is cutting off from the area of feelings altogether; they can seem to be totally cold and hard, and they are incapable of being happy in this state.

The safest thing for Scorpio to do is to be cautious in relationship. As a friendship is tested over time, they then become able to show their feelings in safety. A therapist of some kind may be the very first person that a damaged Scorpio chooses to trust. So Scorpios may have few friendships, but those few will be deep and lasting. One of the deepest areas of sharing in a relationship is sexual expression. For Scorpio there needs to be emotional rapport for satisfaction. Sex for its own sake is not sufficient, as it can be for the more earthy appetites of Taurus.

An image which describes the Scorpio character is the mountain lake which is deep and still. One cannot see what is below the surface and seemingly harmless remarks thrown in, sink without trace. But when the unsuspecting thrower comes that way again, the hurt that has been caused will come out suddenly in unrecognisable form and hit them hard. This is the source of the revenge that Scorpio is known for.

A lake in the mountains can be stagnant and boggy, but if fed by a stream from above, it will remain sweet and overflow to feed the valley below: if Scorpio remembers their spiritual home and draws strength from it, they overflow with understanding and love to support those who suffer.

The spirit in Scorpio is learning to know the emotional depths and accept them, bringing about an inner transformation that also transforms the quality of life. Their consequent wisdom and their understanding of the human condition can be used to assist people who cannot themselves handle their emotions.

♐ Sagittarius "flames"

bursting brightly here and there from a darkening celebration fire, illuminating conversation

By now the spirit has been through each of the elements twice. It has experienced them and learned to handle them. Is it any wonder that in Sagittarius there is the tendency to express a sense of knowing all there is to know?

Here there is the character of the university student, now studying what they choose, working in their own time, sharing endless discussions as to how the world should be run, how well they could run it.

This is the third Fire Sign, where the energy has to be applied for the advance of humanity. The warmth of Fire is expressed in enthusiasm. Sagittarius gets excited about anything that leads to growth and a broader view. All the pieces of information that were gathered in its opposite Sign, Gemini, are put together to form a picture of the universe and all it contains, and the missing bits are the catalyst for explorations, physical and mental.

Sagittarius is the adventurous explorer and philosopher, a student of life. The Sagittarian mind stands on the edge of what is known and leaps, like the excited centaur, intuitively to the next rock, looking back to build a bridge for the concrete mind to follow.

They use both abstract thought and creative imagination to assist in discovering the realms of metaphysics. Because of their insatiable desire to learn and their sometimes wicked sense of humour, they make the most interesting and memorable teachers, inspiring their pupils with the joy of discovery.

In their preoccupation with the need to get the whole picture, they can trample heavy footed over other people's feelings. Their desire to share their bright optimistic humour can lead to tactless jokes, and teasing stories. They may be thoughtless of others' feelings but there will be no intention to hurt. What Sagittarius can bring to the other Signs is a light-heartedness, a reminder that play is the natural balance for serious responsibility.

What the spirit is learning in Sagittarius is the art of seeing pieces of information as parts of the overview of life, and the knack of enthusing others with that vision - passing on the Fire of life in a usable form.

♑ Capricorn "mountain"

firmly broad-based, complex mass accumulating; weathered ancient pathways labouring up to a satisfied rest, rewarded with a distant gaze

As the student in this story leaves college and takes on the responsibility of looking after themselves, so the spirit moves from Sagittarius into Capricorn, the final Earth Sign. Here the experience is of the material world with no-one else responsible but oneself.

The sense of weight for Capricorn is strongest in childhood. It is not easy to open your eyes on a world where you can immediately see what part you are capable of playing. At first there may be a pleasure in the ability to do things well and take charge, but Capricorn children are easily taken for granted in their home situations and responsibility is often heaped upon them without consideration for their child needs of play and affection and caring.

In school some of these children rise to their position of natural authority without loss of popularity, but others, understanding the reason for rules and recognising the difficulties of their class teachers, are often left out of children's games and considered too serious and goody-goody to be one of the gang. So childhood can be lonely and a lot of hard work.

As they get older, the Capricorn characters need to realise that they are responsible only for themselves and their actions, and not for the rest of humanity. Indeed to take responsibility for another can be a way of removing that person's self-respect. It is not easy to feel respect for someone who you consider incapable of managing their own life, even if that person is yourself. At this time we are all learning about being our own masters, taking charge of our own lives, so the best one can do for someone is not to take over, but to encourage them to manage by themselves.

An evolved Capricorn will realise that the material world follows the impulse of energy, and energy follows thought. In this way things are actually achieved in the world through the purposeful application of thought, and through intention. This requires that the limitations of a situation be understood so that any effort will be applied in a useful direction. The steps that will be required for the flowering of the purpose must be in the right order and each one accomplished carefully so that the next step will be steady. If all the laws of nature are obeyed and the purpose is appropriate to the time, success will naturally follow. It can seem to us that their success is a gift or the Capricorn is a magician of some kind, but this is because we are not aware of the care that was involved. What is a magician, after all, but one who accomplishes something in a way that others cannot see or understand.

Capricorn likes to find some purpose in the world which satisfies their need to be useful members of society, and this is often a family. Then their work feeds and clothes the children who need to be cared for while growing. They can regard the people who work for them as their 'family', and a natural and satisfying Capricorn role can be that of 'patriarch' in a company. But as the Capricorn works hard, they will expect their family to take life seriously and work hard as well, so they can be a demanding boss.

In all this work the emotions are not felt to be appropriate, and Capricorn is proud of their ability to put emotions to one side and cope without letting the ups and downs of life interfere. The symbol, Capricornus, is goat at the front and fish behind, showing that the Capricorn character may appear hard and ambitious. The fish's tail, representing their basic wisdom and understanding of life's necessities, is not what they choose to show, perhaps because it is accompanied by a vulnerable sensitivity and emotional responses.

They tend to feel responsibility as a weight, like a large cloak, that they put on at birth. Only as they grow older and more easily able to handle authority, do they discover that the cloak stays the same and is consequently lighter and lighter on their shoulders. No wonder that Capricorns are said to grow younger instead of older, and that their humour becomes light-hearted in later years.

The mountain goat is climbing to survive and be comfortable in the material world. The mountain is the sum of the achievements accrued on the way. At the top of this mountain the spirit has a wide view and a great deal of experience in that world.

The spirit in Capricorn is learning to become the Master of Darkness. There is a danger that the Capricorn natures forget their connection with light, and with it the purpose that makes the work worthwhile and enjoyable. There can grow a moodiness and even depression, and all joy, the hallmark of spirit, evaporates. The task is to be involved with the material world without identifying with it and in this way the natural laws can be applied for the service of the whole.

Aquarius *"bubbles in ice"*

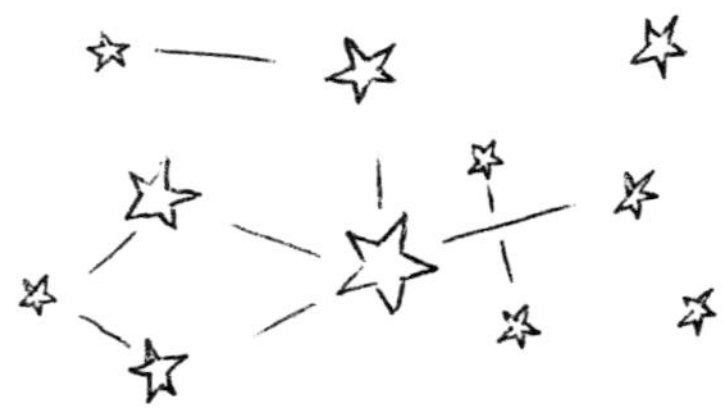

pieces of air caught in permanent relationship, clear, precise, held in awareness together apart

The Zodiac spirit's path becomes Aquarius at the top of Capricorn's mountain of achievement. The members of Capricorn's 'family' have been supported to the point when they can support themselves, and the responsibilities are all fulfilled. Because of past effort there is a sense of inner security and freedom.

The broad view of the world and all past experience gives the spirit in Aquarius the vision to see how society would be best organised to cater for the interests of all individuals. Everyone must have space to be what they want to be, and all must have a fair hearing. Rules are needed to make sure that all runs smoothly and no-one takes advantage of another.

Aquarius, however, often fails to include themself in this organised perfect society. They do not feel bound by the rules, however sensible those rules may be. Another mistake they can make is to assume that all other individuals want what they themselves would want. But not all people require such space, some like to be close to each other, to feel the pull of each other's emotions, unlike the self-contained Aquarius.

Perhaps it is the realisation that emotional reactions upset the smooth running of society, that causes Aquarius to try to ignore them. They tend to overlook the fact that everybody has their own reaction patterns built in from their own past experience. It is as though Aquarius characters have levitated themselves above the sea of emotion and daren't look down in case they fall in.

It is necessary at some point for them to explore their own past and discover the emotions that they fear are lurking there, in order to understand the behaviour of others better. When they understand how others feel, they learn to speak without pouring cold water on new ideas. Their place in society, perhaps as an advisor, becomes clear as they accept the humanness of their own emotional responses.

Here we have the last of the Air Signs, the ability to think and communicate being put to the use of humanity as a whole. Aquarius is usually right in what they say as long as emotions are included in their picture. Sometimes the expectations that Aquarius has of their friends can upset their relationships. While their negative judgement is running, they often demonstrate a complete absence of love, although they will always be willing to mend difficulties with those they consider to be worth the effort.

The idea of love of humanity is very important to Aquarius and without the expression of love, life can be very lonely for them, but they do find individuals very trying. They need to remember that people all have their own priorities. Maybe a Sagittarian friend forgot to send a birthday card, but their love may be demonstrated by a bunch of flowers at some other time of the year. We are all different, but from the great height of Aquarius we all tend to seem the same. Perhaps this is why Aquarians make such an effort to be different from the herd.

The spirit in Aquarius is learning to share their vision of people living in peace world-wide, and to communicate that vision in such a way that it can be manifested by people as they are, with all their emotions catered for.

♓ Pisces ". . . in the sea . . ."

submerged with no reference point, relationship is fluid - what you feel I feel, what you are is me

All other tasks complete, the spirit moves into Pisces, the last of the Water Signs, to give to the sea of humanity what is needed. Pisces is like the monarch who has abdicated the throne in favour of the offspring, and goes out among the people incognito. Here there is no identity except what the moment requires.

Pisces people feel the emotions of the whole human race, particularly those next to them physically or those in mental or psychic contact. They move in a world of emotion where each wave washes them completely, wiping out what was there before. If a depressed person walks past, Pisces feels depressed. If a friend walks in, with a happy smile, Pisces feels happy. They need to be able to distinguish between their own emotions and those of others. With no boundaries to their space, they tend to be sensitive to every person as an invasion. They need to become aware that they are similarly trespassing on other people's space.

Pisces often has difficulty discerning which are the right times to tune in usefully. It is a wonderful ability to sense another's true feelings so that one can react in the most helpful way to that person. But the other half of that ability is to be able to let the emotion through and out again, so that one's judgement is not affected by it, or even to become aware of those emotions before they reach the physical body so they don't upset the Pisces own hormonal system.

Because Pisces bathes in the emotional atmosphere around themselves, they often try to improve it by helping or pleasing others. This can lead to them using up their life energy fulfilling other people's whims and desires. Once they can distinguish between a person's desires and their true growth needs, there is so much work for them, giving comfort to those who have been seriously hurt by their experience, giving assistance to those who are trying to move forward in their lives.

What the spirit is learning in Pisces is the ability to remain consciously aware in the present moment, even in the depths of humanity's emotions; aware of the difference between emotions generated from within and possibly reflecting back, and those that are truly another's. Consciousness is needed in every atom of creation for all to be truly a part of that great Oneness, and Pisces is the channel through which the Light of consciousness can flow into creation, so that all can be healed by the truth.

Perhaps it is easier now to understand why the spirit in Aries bursts into a new realisation of individuality with such force, after the memory of being so vastly undefined!

The Zodiac

Part 2

Ways in which we are different

Tropical versus Sidereal Zodiac - a bit of astronomy

When people talk about the Zodiac in magazines, newspapers and Western astrology books, they are referring to twelve equal divisions of the sky starting at the position of the Sun at the Spring Equinox, which is called '0° Aries'. They are not actually referring to that belt of stars wrapped round the earth like a massive girdle and divided into twelve or thirteen unequally sized constellations.

In the West we use the Tropical Zodiac, so-called because it has named the Tropics of Cancer and Capricorn. Geographically, the area on the globe known as the 'tropics' is defined as the belt round the earth either side of the equator, which extends North to the line of latitude called the Tropic of Cancer, where the sun is directly overhead at the Solstice in June, and South to the Tropic of Capricorn, where the sun is directly overhead at the Solstice in December.

Hindu astrology, used in India, is based on the Sidereal Zodiac which is twelve equal Signs derived from the distant constellations. It tells the same story as any cycle in twelve parts, the same story as the Tropical Zodiac, but the emphasis of the Sidereal Zodiac is on the relationship of the earth directly with the cosmos in its entirety; whereas the Tropical Zodiac is concerned with the relationship between life on Earth and the Sun as our life-giving centre of the solar system.

Psychologically perhaps this is an aspect of the difference between the attitudes to life in the East and West, apparent also in the religions. In the East we are seen as beings relating to space, the universe, our goal being to lose our sense of self entirely in the Oneness. In the West we tend to see ourselves as personality in relationship with God as a single Source of life, like the Sun.

I like to blend the two aims, so we would first endeavour to shift our identity from personality (the Earth and Moon) to personal spiritual source (the Sun), and then recognise the 'spark of divinity' within each of us as a bridge to conscious divine Oneness.

Practitioners of Hindu, or Vedic, astrology, with all its precise rules, can be adept at prediction, whereas the Tropical Zodiac is used more as a psychological tool to assist character analysis and personal development. The bias of my interpretation is towards seeing how our experience of life is a reflection of our character so that, through acceptance and love of it all, we may expand beyond personality limitations into spiritual dimensions.

The Tropical, or Western, Zodiac always aligns 0 degrees Aries with the position of the sun at that Equinox which falls in Spring in the Northern Hemisphere. The rest of the Western Zodiac is measured from that point, dividing the circle into twelve Signs of 30° each. The Spring and Autumn Equinoxes are those moments in the year when the day and night are of equal length and, as the Earth rolls on its axis, the sun appears to rise exactly due East.

In the days following the Spring Equinox the Sun will be rising ever further North of East until at the Summer Solstice when it is in 0° Cancer, it rises at its furthest

North, directly over the Tropic of Cancer on the Earth. After the Autumn Equinox the sun will rise further South until at the Winter Solstice it will be over the Tropic of Capricorn.

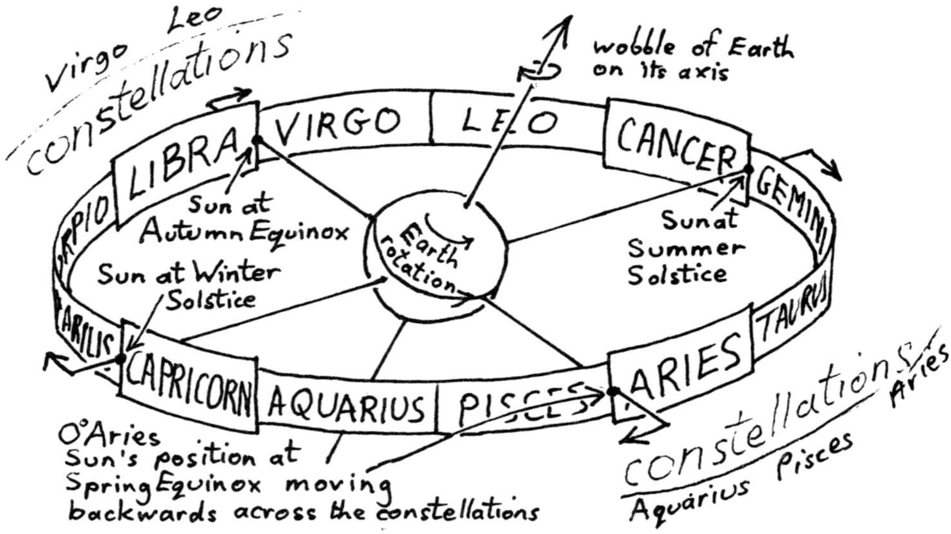

Due to the wobble of the earth's axis as it revolves, the Spring Equinox point of 0° Aries moves slowly backwards through the constellations. Every 25,000 years or so the two Zodiacs, Sidereal and Tropical, are aligned: that is to say, behind the sun at the Spring Equinox is the beginning of the Aries constellation, so that 0° Aries will be moving backwards into Pisces again.

The last time the Zodiacs were aligned was the period of Jesus' life, which was the end of the Age of Aries and the beginning of the Age of Pisces: Jesus, the Lamb of the Aries Ram, was gathering his disciples, 'fishers of men' to teach love and service, Pisces attributes.

Having travelled backwards through the Pisces constellation, the Spring Equinox point is now in the area of sky between the constellations of Pisces and Aquarius. The precise point of change between constellations is not agreed upon, so there tends to be dispute as to exactly when the Age of Aquarius starts.

This 'new age', will be concerned with using the fruit of Pisces to bring about a perfect Aquarian condition. Perhaps the ideal has been to let go of our personalities and blend with the boundless love of Pisces through service to each other, and now, in Aquarius, we are to discover individually the truth of our spiritual identity. As spirit is boundary-less, spiritually all is one, and maybe in Aquarius 'I' can become consciously one with life's unity while still occupying an individual body on earth. Anyway we have two thousand-odd years to get the message!

All this makes a fascinating study but it is not necessary to know it, in order to practise astrological chart reading, so we will continue to explore the Tropical Zodiac Signs.

Each Sign has its difficulty

There is always someone we know who shows us the negative side of their own Sun-Sign. Aries attacks, Taurus is lazy, Virgo is critical, Scorpio is vindictive! Every Sign has its negative side. What we need to know is how it feels to be that Sign when the negative behaviour is what they are doing: why do they do that?

The following are little suggestions as to what is going on inside such negative behaviour. If we can understand how it feels inside, we will be able to have a more helpful response.

♈ **Aries** is learning how to use energy - they often get it wrong. They are glad when people stand up to them because they don't intend to hurt or destroy. They need to be encouraged or they can become unsure and depressed. They begin new things, or revive things that were thought to be over, and they feel the need to keep moving on to the next.

♉ **Taurus** at heart is silent, prefering to commune with Nature. Being so in touch with earth energy, they can heal others with it. They can seem slow or lazy but they need time to feel secure before they can speak or act. They tend to use no more energy than it takes to achieve something, and they appreciate the value of leisure.

♊ **Gemini**'s difficulty is linking the two halves of the brain. When in the left brain mode (rational) they think and talk well - when in the right brain (intuitive) they are silent, not knowing how to communicate it. They need to accept and express the imaginative, creative side.

♋ **Cancer,** by its nature, feels emotions like waves on the sea - up and down and up again. They need to be given time to come back up. Cancer people are part parent - part child, and need to learn to mother their own inner neediness, otherwise they will get someone else to play one of these parts, and feel possessive of them.

♌ **Leo** is mostly front. It is easy to crush them with coolness. It takes much courage and energy to radiate so much, and they need lots of love and smiles from others to keep it going. They need to listen as well as radiate, and it is not easy to do both at the same time. If appreciated, they will do anything for you.

Virgo criticises themselves more than anyone else, feeling that anything short of perfection is not good enough. They give themselves a very hard time. They often tell only the fault, forgetting to voice their more appreciative thoughts. They thrive on being recognised as helpful and will assist you if you tell them how their talents can be useful. ♍

Libra is afraid to upset the balance. When they have all the facts about a situation, they will recognise what is the best thing to do, but not before. The only decision they can make quickly is one they know doesn't really matter, but deciding whether a decision is in that class may take some time. They lift what others cast down. ♎

Scorpio is emotionally vulnerable at a deeper level than the other Signs. They use many methods of protection: silence, directing attention at other people, being prickly to keep others at bay. As they explore and accept their own emotions, they become able to understand and support others through the worst disasters. ♏

Sagittarius may not be able to prove what they know, or say how they know it. Their imagination takes them beyond the rational, and their teaching creates a linking bridge. Their enthusiasm is intended to inspire others to make their own efforts, not to lead them. Their natural good humour can produce jokes that offend others unintentionally. ♐

Capricorn carries responsibility like a cloak. It is heavy for a child but feels lighter as they get older. Their innate knowledge of the physical makes their achievements seem magical. The pleasing results of their hard work matters more to them than emotional expression, so they often omit to tell people when they are feeling overburdened. ♑

♒ **Aquarius** may seem cool but they are levitating over a sea of emotion which threatens to engulf them if they look down. Their detachment gives them wonderful vision, but it will exclude the feeling aspect of humanity unless they have looked into their own sea. Their strong attachment to principles can lead them to be hurt by others with different priorities.

♓ **Pisces** has no boundaries, which is difficult in the material world. They need to learn to make personal boundaries in order to know what they are feeling. When centred in their hearts they can identify with spirit itself, which knows no boundaries.

Exercise:

1 Check inside yourself to see how you feel when you express the negative of your own Sun-Sign.

2 Ask your friends how they are feeling when they act negatively.

Negative opposites to Sun-Signs

It is interesting to look at the people you know in terms of their Sun-Sign. The Sun represents the quality of a person's spiritual radiance, if they give their spirit the opportunity to radiate by expressing the Sign.

When a person's spirit is being expressed, they will show quite strong characteristics of their Sun-Sign: positive when feeling good, and negative when in difficulty. Positive or negative, the whole personality is holding together, and their light is shining even though it may feel uncomfortable to others. You would say of the person that they were reasonably well-integrated and there will be a light in their eyes.

If this is not the case, the personality will be scattered and the person will feel every obstacle as a great hurdle to be overcome, instead of being just the next thing to deal with. There are many ways of being less than our best and they are all part of being human. However, when a person starts to behave like the negative of the Sign *opposite* their Sun-Sign, it shows that they are having difficulty being themselves, operating from the heart. This opposite Sign will be behind the earth and is sometimes called the Earth-Sign. It indicates the personality without its spirit, so it is a Sign of darkness.

For instance, an **Aries ♈** person who is not expressing either force, energy, aggressiveness or impatience, who is not starting new projects with great zeal - will tend to seem all "yes, but -", wishy-washy and indecisive, i.e. negative **Libra ♎**. A **Pisces ♓** person who is not being sensitive, looking after someone else in some way, expressing their emotions or reflecting the emotions of others - will often show themselves as cold perfectionists with a tendency to criticise, i.e. negative **Virgo ♍**.

A person who is expressing their negative-opposite state is very possibly out of touch with their Sun-Sign and, if that is so, life will be more difficult for them than is necessary. Great help can be given in a chart reading by showing in a sensitive way, how the person can change their behaviour or thought processes very slightly, tipping the balance back towards their own Sign.

When we are moved to help a friend to feel better, we tend to go about it in ways which would make *us* feel better, but each Sun-Sign has their own needs. If you know your friend's Sun-Sign, you can, in daily conversation, encourage them to 'be themselves' (their Sign) more. Such a change will naturally lead to behaviour that opens the door to their own spirit, which can then express again through their personality. Their light comes on again and life starts to flow more easily.

The following are some of the negative traits of opposite Signs, accompanied by a few possible ways to bring the person back to their own Sun-Sign. Many more ways could be found. It takes not only knowing something of the Signs but also a good knowledge of the individual character, to find the right way for that person - the wrong way can just make matters worse!

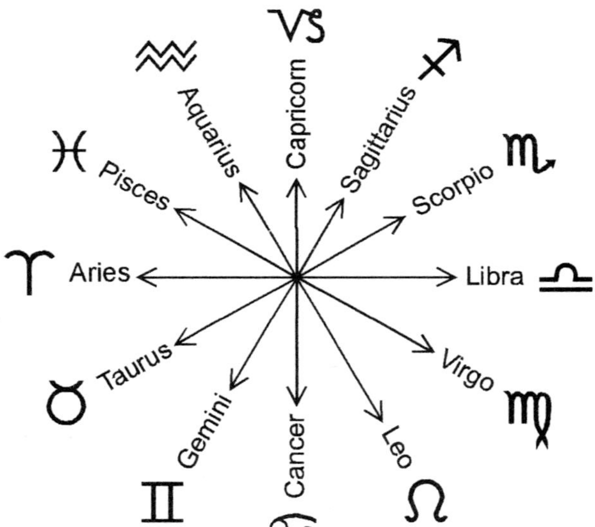

♈ **Aries**, when afraid to act, or staggering from a perceived attack, can become **negative Libra** - indecisive, worried, inactive, going on about different possibilities without enthusiasm, "yes, but . . ." etc.
To bring them back to their Aries heart centre suggest - "just do what you want to do", "do it your own way", "you can do it!" . . .

Taurus, when feeling unsteady, uncertain or unsafe, or having lost a treasured possession, can become **negative Scorpio** - angry, seething, hurtful statements, blaming, vengeful, etc. ♉
To bring them back to their Taurus heart centre suggest - a walk in the park together, a meal out, a day in the country, a massage . . .

Gemini, when feeling unable to think or communicate, can become **negative Sagittarius** - head in the clouds, can't be bothered to explain, witty jokes at another's expense, wanting to get away, etc. ♊
To bring them back to their Gemini heart centre suggest - "what have you heard about . . . (something topical) ?", "read anything interesting lately?", ask them to tell you what the problem is . . .

Cancer, when feeling unloved, or heavily responsible for their loved ones, can become **negative Capricorn** - getting on with their work huffily, "I've got all this work to do", "the world's going down-hill" etc. ♋
To bring them back to their Cancer heart centre - put your arm around their shoulders, ask what has upset them, listen and don't try to put things right . . .

Leo, when feeling lack of energy, or when rebuffed or hurt, can become **negative Aquarius** - keeping away from people, wont say how they feel, apathetic etc. ♌
To bring them back to their Leo heart centre - tell them what you like about their warmth, verbally appreciate something about their appearance or their style, smile into their eyes, help them laugh about something . . .

♍ **Virgo**, when feeling unable to cope, or when their helpful intentions are misunderstood, can become **negative Pisces** - emotional, unfocussed, 'martyred', weepy, feeling useless etc.
To bring them back to their Virgo heart centre suggest - "what would you advise me to do about (something they are good at) ?", "you really organised . . . well", point out how truly helpful they are, say "How can I help you?" . . .

♎ **Libra**, when feeling challenged or criticised, or feeling pressured to make a decision, can become **negative Aries** - aggressive, argumentative, etc.
To bring them back to their Libra heart centre suggest - "take your time", "what colour would best describe how you feel?", "how can these two viewpoints be reconciled?", play music they like . . .

♏ **Scorpio**, when feeling exposed and vulnerable, or deeply hurt, can become **negative Taurus** - stubbornly silent, obstructive etc.
To bring them back to their Scorpio heart centre suggest - "it may be hard to put into words, but can you tell me how you are feeling?", or, if you can accept it, let them express their anger, grief or pain, or point out the funny side . . .

♐ **Sagittarius**, when feeling trapped by responsibility, or becoming overstretched with commitments, can become **negative Gemini** - flippant, superficial, talking without meaning, upset and not talking at all, etc.
To bring them back to their Sagittarius heart centre - ask which of their commitments have the highest priority, ask "Is there an adventure here in disguise?", suggest an outing or party . . .

Capricorn, when feeling overburdened with responsibilities and unsupported, can become **negative Cancer** - moody, possessive, emotional ♑
To bring them back to their Capricorn heart centre suggest - "I really appreciate all the work you are doing", "it is wonderful how one can rely on you doing what you say you will do", "That was a great achievement (something they worked hard at)", "What are you upset about?" . . .

Aquarius, when losing their detached point of view about something, can become **negative Leo** - dogmatic, domineering, not listening etc. ♒
To bring them back to their Aquarian heart centre suggest - "why do you think that happened?", "you sound a bit involved, could you say what it is that's getting to you?, ask in a group, "What do you others think about that?", answer the words they spoke not their tone of voice . . .

Pisces, when feeling taken for granted, or exhausted from caring for someone, can become **negative Virgo** - cold, critical, perfectionist etc. ♓
To bring them back to their Pisces heart centre suggest - "do you ever get the feeling no-one appreciates you?", "it must be really difficult sometimes being as sensitive as you are", "what's the worst of the situation?" and encourage them to have a good cry, or moan, about it to let it out of the system, ask what boundaries they feel they need . . .

Important Note:

When any person (including yourself) is acting out the negative of their *own* Sun-Sign, there is no need to interfere. They do not need help, just the opportunity to express themselves without being judged!

Also, most people feel better when someone is prepared to give them some undivided attention, and listen to them telling what is going on, without interrupting or trying to solve their problems for them.

Perhaps the most important point about the Zodiac Signs is that every person feels better about themselves when the gifts of their own Sun Sign are appreciated by others. If we would appreciate children when they are expressing their Sun Sign qualities, they would have a better sense of self-esteem, a better start in life.

Exercises:

1 Think about times when you act the negative of your opposite Sign. What would bring you back?

2 Notice a friend during negative behaviour. Is it the negative of their own Sun-Sign, or the opposite? If it is the opposite, how do you think they would be best helped back to their own Sign? Does it work? If not, why not?

3 What does work?

Chapter 3
The Planets

Part 1
Ways in which we are the same

For speed and simplicity we usually refer to the Sun, Moon and planets, as 'the planets'. We will be focus on the planets in different ways to encourage all aspects of the mind to be involved, and also to assist the memory.

The 'Seven Sacred Planets' as Chakras

Spirit is all there is. It manifests as the essence of life and, as vibration, could be described as Light. Mentally it is pure consciousness; it feels to us like love, the force of attraction that holds all forms; it appears to us as physical experience. So we say that the entire universe is irradiated by the Light. It is so intense that, for most of us, awareness of it in our daily lives just as it is, would leave us unable to function as a *personality* unless we were well prepared.

As we generally identify ourselves with our separate personality, we tend to fear personal annihilation and protect ourselves from this Light. Reflecting that protection, the Earth's atmosphere slows down the vibration of life energy for us, and splits it into a spectrum of 'colours', each colour having a different *function*.

We can then experience the Light like a rainbow flowing through our bodies, expressing every level of existence possible at the same time. In each area of the body, the whirling vortex of energy has manifested a bunch of nerve tissue, a nerve plexus, to channel one of the functions necessary to the process of living. These vortices, or energy centres, are sometimes called chakras, meaning wheels. So the energy flowing through each chakra expresses every level of existence relevant to the function of that area of the body, from physical, through emotional, mental and spiritual, to the reality of Oneness, the Source of life. These functions of energy are reflected in many other ways throughout our bodies, our lives, our world, and every experience of which we are capable.

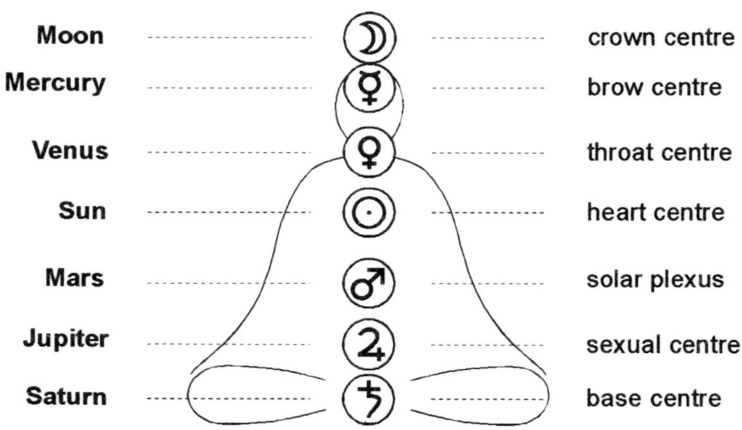

The planets surrounding Earth also represent the different functions on all levels, in the same way as do the chakras. Traditionally the seven planets chosen to match the seven chakras involved in alchemical spiritual training are the Sun and Moon, and those planets that could be seen before telescopes were invented. Mercury, Venus, Mars, Jupiter and Saturn look just like stars twinkling different colours and degrees of brightness, but over the weeks they can be seen to 'wander' through the fixed star patterns.

There are different systems for locating the planets in the body, and systems of meaning for the chakras, and there are different systems of arrangement of chakras in the body. What is important is to select the system you will use like a grid, through which to look at experience. Never be seduced into thinking one system is 'the way things truly are' and another 'wrong'. One learns with practice to 'read' experience through one's chosen grid. Each person's experience is what it is for them; different grids just express it differently, or show a different perspective. In this system the seven planetary energies can be said to correspond with seven of the major chakras in the following way *(the colours that indicate health in that area are in brackets)*:

crown centre **Moon** *(amethyst)* - ☽
energy of universal spirit for responding, and playing with creation

brow centre **Mercury** *(indigo)* - ☿
mental energy for vision and communication

throat centre **Venus** *(sky blue)* - ♀
attracting energy for balancing and relating

heart centre **Sun** *(green)* - ☉
consciousness of essential Self for understanding and love

solar plexus **Mars** *(yellow)* - ♂
emotional energy for effective action and control

sexual centre **Jupiter** *(orange)* - ♃
expansive energy for growth and compassion

base centre **Saturn** *(red)* - ♄
consolidating energy for stability and perseverance

All creation is only possible if there is 'separation from the Source'. If there is no separation from source - if everything *is* source - then the concepts of 'creation' and 'time' have no real meaning. So let us play with them, and imagine the moment of creation as a process in time. That process reflected in the head and spine of our body, might appear as a ripple of movement from Oneness at the crown through many levels of creation to the physical world at the base. If the spine is aligned when the Light of the Source is received by the Moon at the crown centre, it strikes the base so that Saturn, as Lucifer, the Light Bringer, is able to shed that light on our path through physical life, teaching us through experience.

Balancing the chakras

If each of the seven chakras from the base up, or the crown down, is one of the seven colours of the rainbow, balancing and combining them would give us white light. When our balanced system can produce white light we are tuned to the universal Light of pure spirit, Unity, Oneness.

Exercise: *A meditation to balance the chakra energies*

Having organised a space for yourself to be on your own, sit quietly with your back comfortably straight and imagine the seven centres as described, as globes on your spine, inside your body, starting with the base for good stability during the exercise. As you focus on each one, imagine it the relevant colour of the rainbow. When all seven are alight, check over and over them until all centres are radiating their colour with the same intensity of light. If this is difficult, try putting an image of your spine and centres out in front of you and balance the colours there. It will be just as effective. Let spiritual Light enter your crown centre. Be sure you are safely in your body at the end.

Planets as human characteristics

Usually you will find the planets listed with Sun and Moon first as the two lights of our life, by day and by night. The others are given afterwards in order of their normal distance from, and speed of rotation round, the sun.

The following descriptions are in that order, written in the first person as if describing the experience of the reader's spirit. Listening with your imagination as well as your intellect will key your mind in to the greater meaning of each planet and each corresponding principle of life:

"Before starting the journey into material life, there is a state of Oneness which is what I am eternally. Nothing has ever happened, nor ever will, to affect my true state, because in eternity there is no time. Then, by my choice to incarnate, I set in motion the effects of separation which include time, development, growth, process, path and so on.

From the moment of conception I am growing, reflected by the spiralling dance of Earth, planets and the whole cosmos. I transform as a foetus through every stage of evolution of life during my nine months in the womb. At birth, I stop growing in this way, I take my stand, choose my personality for this life, and the reflected picture is shown in my birth chart."

Sun (heart centre) our essential character. ☉

"I choose a Sun-Sign for the heart where my spirit will come through into Earth experience. Here is where I will be aware of my Higher Self or spirit when I am not too caught up in identifying with my personality. At first. it is clear and uncluttered. When I am open and honest, it is radiant with understanding and love."

(The relationship of the Sun to the rest of the birth chart shows what experiences tend to cover our heart with pain and what can help to keep them clear. See: 'Planets Part II, Ways in which we are different'.)

☽ **Moon** (crown centre) our personal unconscious.

"The Earthly experience begins with mother who is necessary to me, who is all the world to me, reflected by the Moon-Sign, the light in the darkness of night, the dual and changeable nature of Earthly life being the dark as opposed to the daylight of spiritual unity.

"The Moon-Sign is the baby and child that I act out, fettered by all my expectations from so much projected experience in past lives. Out of them, I develop survival aids before I am old enough to think consciously, so my reactions to mother, as well as mother's own feelings and thoughts, are a large part of these unconscious assumptions and behaviour.

"I need to be in touch with the spirit love-light in order to shine, and at first I am in touch with it (or not) through my mother. Yet, as I grow I tend to continue looking for it outside me in the Earthly world - from my mother to any other context in which I find myself.

"Instead of remembering my contact with the light of the universe via the crown chakra, I stack my unconscious here, with all my forgotten experiences, habit patterns and prejudices, blocking the light. As I become self-aware by shining the light of consciousness into the unknown areas of myself, I shift these personal blockages at the crown chakra and it becomes a clear opening, receptive to the spiritual light of the universe."

(The placing of Moon in the birth chart shows what we expect, and so attract, from our mothers and our world.)

Mercury (brow centre) our mind and its access point between the brain's frontal lobes. ☿

"Through my body, my senses, I learn about my world, and then discover that it responds to me. So I begin communication with the mother and with all other surroundings. It is from this centre that I can see out and communicate with clarity, without moral judgment. However, my habits of thought and my preoccupations, both conscious and semi-conscious, tend to come from one side of my brain or the other and cloud the central view.

"Mercury links Moon and Venus, as the symbol indicates: the link between our habitual expectations (Moon ☽) and our relationship with the outside (Venus ♀). So it refers to the forming of words to speak or write in order to make that link. When I am aware of the present, it represents clear conscious vision and intuitive grasp and brings the conscious understanding that I am free to change the way I see things."

(Mercury's position in the chart will show both how we give and receive mental communications most naturally, and also what helps us to think clearly.)

Venus (throat centre) our personal love. ♀

"As a baby, I am love, I live on love as a need. I am in relationship with everything I experience as an extension of myself, therefore everything is love - but love of the kind that I am predisposed to think I deserve. This is the attracting energy that draws people together, and if I can accept that people are the way they are, without thinking that I know what that is, the radiation of this centre creates harmony and beauty in my social life. When balanced, its expression is through service. Otherwise I may use it to cover up my negative and acquisitive feelings with false smiles and praise that is out of place. When I want particular reactions from people, the energy stops going out from me. Then I feel needy and become an emotional vacuum which can only attract other vacuums, no-one fulfilling the needs of anyone else."

(Venus and her Sign, House, and connections with the other planetary energies, all show how this loving functions in our world, how it gets distorted and by what. It also shows the way love needs to be expressed for us to recognise that love is what we are being given.)

♂ **Mars** (solar plexus) our reservoir of emotional energy which is what gives power to thoughts, and makes an intention effective.

"As a baby, at first I have no sense of being able to do anything specific to survive. Gradually it dawns on me that different actions have different effects. I try to do what will get what I need, and later, as experience teaches me, to get what I want (because wants can feel like needs to a child). This is Mars, the motivating force of desire, that acts to be effective, to get what is wanted. It is my motive force, helping me to reach out and control what I see around me.

"It is also here that I am most sensitive to psychic and emotional atmospheres. I need to be careful not to allow myself to be overly affected by how I think others are thinking and feeling, because that keeps me from being aware of my own true state.

"To help and heal another, it is necessary for me to be in contact with, and channel, the energy of Oneness. Channelling that energy as helpfully as possible is done most effectively through the open heart or the clear mind. At the solar plexus, energy is more likely to be personalised with my own drive for survival and will tend to pass those concerns to the recipient of my desire to heal. My Mars centre supplies energy for me. When healthy, it will supply the energy *I* need to accomplish *my* intentions, deal with circumstances as they happen, and radiate sufficiently to keep me centred."

(The chart position of Mars shows the old survival programming from which we operate, which sometimes determines that we assert ourselves in ways that we expect to work even though, in practice, they don't. It also indicates which activities in our lives spark our energy most and where we tend to waste it, or lose it, unconsciously.)

The above five are called the personal planets. The next two planets could be called socialising influences, because they represent the characteristics that lead us to be concerned about, and involved with, other people even when we have nothing personal to gain.

Jupiter (sexual centre) our growth, through the creative energy of enjoyment, expanding to include everything. ♃

"As the baby that I am becomes better able to control this bodily equipment, eyes and hands, I expand by stretching out beyond myself and taking in what is new. I discover that there is much that I cannot move directly (that which is not my body) and using the Jupiter function I explore the rest of my world, thereby growing and achieving a broader understanding.

"As an adult, I need to be relaxed at this centre, feeling free to enjoy the gifts of the universe without losing myself in indulgence or expecting the rest of society to feed me. From a state of having and deserving abundance, I will feel able to give interest, care and encouragement generously to those I meet. Through the sexual centre I create experiences in the physical world that expand me - including having babies! Using this same energy in higher mental activity, I expand my understanding to include new ideas and concepts. By forgetting myself and the fear that holds me back, I stretch out to take the shape of my potential."

(Of the many experiences we have, we will judge some as pleasant and some as not pleasant and, according to our expectations, which Jupiter's chart placing shows, we will tend to go forward and work with them, or recoil and maybe even expect someone else to make things better for us.)

♄ **Saturn** (base centre) our sense of stability, whether as a separate being or as part of the whole, and the difficulties we experience when we identify with anything other than our Source.

"Some of the experiences I have in early life seem to teach me things that are inexorable whatever I do. These are Saturn experiences, where I learn about the boundaries that define my world. Any structure of its nature is restricting; edges, boundaries, definitions are all limits of energy or thought that enable manifestation. Any path has edges, and without a path or guidance my personality would wander, lost.

"The difficulty I have with limits is my tendency to identify with them as part of how I need to be. I tend not to realise that every situation expresses its own limits which may not apply to other situations. Recognising this, I realise that I am free to make my own rules about my life as long as I take complete responsibility for everything I perceive as being round me or happening to me. Until then, I identify as Saturn the people involved in teaching me discipline, and I feel them imposing limits and controlling me.

"Only gradually (if ever) will I learn to take responsibility for, and discipline, myself. As I realise how my experience of circumstances is influenced by what attitude I hold, the fear of arbitrary rebuffs abates, and I become able to learn from my experiences. This knowledge gives me a natural authority in my life. At this centre I am careful in building my foundations in the world, to create maximum stability and safety. This requires steadfast perseverance, intelligent patience and wise flexibility."

(Saturn's relationship with the rest of our birth chart describes how we react to rules and laws, including the people who manage them, or our own self-discipline. Saturn also shows how we tend to behave in response to them as developed through all our past experiences.)

We need every one of these seven aspects of energy in life. For instance, on the one hand the expansive generosity of **Jupiter** which we love to receive and feel, would deplete our reserves if we paid no attention to our own structural needs, **Saturn**. On the other hand the steadfast perseverance of Saturn can be without value if it is not guided by a vision of possibilities that Jupiter gives.

Again, **Venus** is the personal love principle, creating harmony between people and in society, yet without the energy of **Mars**, nothing would get done and society would collapse. Considered from the other direction, it would be all very well achieving whatever you set out to achieve with Mars, but without Venus to mediate there may be no-one around when you need them.

Also, **Mercury** represents our ability to think and analyse, yet there is a ceiling to our understanding unless we are open to the rest of existence through the **Moon**. However, spiritual connection through the Moon centre may be wonderful but, to translate it into everyday wisdom, we need the function of Mercury.

These six energies might seem to cover the entire human experience, but our personalities struggle to survive the requirements of every day when they are without the **Sun**, the heart centre, radiating the light and life of who we are into all we do.

Exercise: *A meditation to set the purposes for each of the chakra energies*

Sit comfortably in a space where you know you will not be disturbed for a while. How you begin is up to you, do whatever you find brings you to a state of physical relaxation and bright awareness. One way to do this is: with your back straight but not under strain, let the muscles relax on the out-breath in a wave from the head and neck, through shoulders down to your feet. As you breath in, allow Earth energy to rise from your feet to the base of your spine and, in a wave upwards, allow each bone in your back to lift upwards, balancing your head lightly on the top. Breath for a while relaxing and lifting.

♄ When you feel ready, focus on the base chakra and be aware of the Saturn sense of stability, reliability and inner strength dissolving all fear.

♃ Lifting the energy of your awareness to the sexual centre, feel Jupiter released from fear and enjoy the expansion of creative possibilities. Rather than letting the energy sink down, hold it as compassion for humanity and then draw it up with your awareness into the large solar plexus centre.

Here feel Mars filling the reservoir ready for appropriate action to be directed from higher up. As the energy builds, lift it to the heart centre. ♂

There it lights the flame in the centre of the Sun which bursts into a glorious golden radiance. Bask in the light from the heart until you feel your whole body and space glowing, know that your true self is in residence. ☉

Then, with your awareness, follow that light up to your throat centre where Venus may want to sound a note, hum, or tell you some words that you need to express later, perhaps to someone else. Feel the Venus quality of gentleness and beauty smoothing the energy into a fine upward stream to the centre of your head. ♀

Now let Mercury pull it forward into the middle of your forehead, the brow centre and in the flame that burns there feel yourself waiting, poised, looking and listening with clarity. ☿

While you remain with Mercury in the brow, feel a stream of energy from the centre of your head move upwards to the crown centre, and there relax and allow the Moon to open into fullness. With silver light glowing in the universe and showering over you, awake to contact with All-That-Is. ☽

When you come back down gently close each centre of awareness to a point. Imagine your personal space the size you want it to be and secure before you get up, and remember to be in touch with our constant support system of Mother Earth and Spirit.

This meditation can be combined with the previous one where you balanced the chakras.

The Outer Planets

The rest of the planets, sometimes referred to as transpersonal or trans-Saturnians, beyond Saturn, are considered as life principles and, in this system of correspondences, do not relate specifically to centres in the body. They will be described in order of their discovery. I like to relate to them as great guides, each explaining to us their particular life principle and helping us to integrate it through our experiences.

♅ **Uranus** is teaching us about the principle of freedom.

The fact that Uranus is part of the solar system, indicates that we need not feel ourselves confined by the Saturn boundaries, the laws as we saw them in childhood. We can break free from past ways, we can stand clear of family programming, we are capable of changing our expectations, we can observe our emotional habits.

We notice a desire for freedom when we are feeling trapped. We often trap ourselves by taking more responsibility than is useful, or by being 'nice' to people in the mistaken belief that it helps them more than speaking our truth would do. We have tended to think that we must separate from something or someone in order to be free but, through the Uranian experience of cutting off, we discover that, however often we free ourselves from the outside world, we still feel the same inside. We are still trapping ourselves through our thoughts about life and consequently our behaviour.

Gradually we learn that freedom is an inner sense, and we can achieve it without separation from the outside. It is the ability to be involved in situations without identifying ourselves with any single viewpoint or person or emotion or outcome. If we are swayed by judgement about whether we like something or not, we restrict our freedom of choice. Similarly, if we identify with one thing, we are separate from the rest. Inner freedom enables us to see clearly an entire situation including ourselves, and in that state we can feel compassion for everybody.

Uranian energy is electrical, the energy most appropriate to our nervous system. When we experience a sudden change in some aspect of our life, Uranus is waking us to new insights or to an exciting vision of how things could be, tempting us out of the rut we fall into through Saturn activities.

(The chart position indicates where we tend to want to take our freedom, and therefore where issues around being trapped show up. Its connections to other planets show how comfortable we are with the principle of separation from people, or whether abandonment is feared.)

Neptune is teaching us about the oneness of all life. ♆

We were part of it before we separated into a personality and, in the longing for that state, we try to merge with others in our world. Neptune dissolves the boundaries between things and people so that we experience merging with that which is not ourself. Without any boundaries at all, the material world of form disappears and there is only light, spirit, all is One. The process towards this spiritual meditative state is a confusing one, because the boundaries are removed gradually one by one, faded out. Our experience of this process involves gradually realizing that things are not what they seemed before, and that we know more than we did but that knowledge is not provable. In discovering what is revealed we realize that we have made mistakes in judgment and we experience feelings of let down, deception and even betrayal. On one level we intuit the truth about people, but we do not always take notice of that level.

As we get used to each level of subtlety, we experience ourselves as being more psychic, intuitive or spiritual depending which layer has just been removed. It is easy to lose touch with the results and get sidetracked into the easiest way of merging for us, like alcohol or drugs or even attachment to a particular kind of meditation, or a particular guru. When people discover the psychic world they often get stuck in the glamour of the abilities and fail to push through. Dissolve a few more veils and we can merge with the beauty, love and joy of spirit itself.

Through our efforts to re-unite with Oneness, we eventually realize that we need to dissolve that which we thought we were. We come to see that we never really separated, and that all is still as it was and always will be, one wholeness. We realize that in thinking of ourselves as if we were our personality, we obscure this truth.

(Neptune shows us, in its chart placing, the pitfalls of the particular way we tend to merge, and where we can trust our perceptions. It shows us how to merge again with Oneness and know that is our true identity.)

♇ **Pluto** is teaching us about the attitude required to allow transformation of our core identity from personality to spirit. Its discovery indicates that such transformation in the human mind has become possible.

Our first use of that power tends to involve efforts to dominate through direct control or manipulation before we realise that it is not possible to change what is outside us. We can, however, change ourselves. Change that is lasting has to be from the roots up, which means that something in us has to die. It is this death that we fear. We know what we would like to have and what we wish to lose, but we cannot be sure ahead of time what is really out-of-date. So we cling to the past which feels secure even though it restricts our growth, and it is this very clinging that makes Pluto transformations so painful.

When we open our heart to let go of everything, only that which has no life in the present, that which we have outgrown, falls away. Pluto's principle uproots us, shakes off our habits and comfortable yet unhelpful relationships, trims the roots that depend on the past, and replants us in fresh circumstances that will enable us to develop our potential. After the changes are complete, all that is relevant to us is still there and also much more than we ever dreamed was possible. This entire experience can be intense and feels extremely important at the time. All that we have swept under the carpet and pretended we could hide, comes out into the open. Emotions will not be hidden, words we have held back come out like lava from a volcano. Life is overturned, but as the old behaviour patterns are destroyed we find our true power and can identify more with who we truly are.

(Pluto's position in relation to the rest of the charted personality shows where we tend to hold onto control most obsessively because that is where the transformation could occur. That place is like the hole in the fabric, the present moment of Now, that, if we can get into it totally, reveals eternity. So Pluto's chart position shows where we tend to hold back and therefore feel like victims of another's power.)

Chiron (pronounced in English, 'kyron'), has an odd, comet-like orbit. It was discovered in 1977 between the orbits of Saturn (structures) and Uranus (freedom) and this gives us much of its meaning as used in astrology.

⚷ **Chiron** is teaching us that we are not separate from each other, and that the moment we reach beyond our pain to give to another, our wounds begin to heal.

We can know Oneness, and yet we continually find ourselves separate in our daily experience. Our spirit knows that, while in Earth, it is our effort to defend our sense of woundedness that separates us from others. The Chiron experience is of being damaged at birth so it seems the trauma happens then or before. It is an area where we lack confidence or even feel that we are completely useless. At first, those more compassionate children try to help other people in that area of experience, but on some occasion their help will be rejected and the pain of the old wound is triggered.

It feels as though everyone conspires to make us feel bad and we may lash out at them; what we say out of our pain will be true and aimed straight for the other person's wound, whether we are aware of that or not. We somehow expect to be hurt so we feel the need to protect ourselves by avoiding those people or situations where hurt occurs. We wall ourselves around with negative statements of what we cannot achieve, what we could not possibly do, and at first it feels safe; if we do not attempt things, then we cannot fail. Gradually we grow inside the self-made boundaries until we feel imprisoned. We are afraid that if we step outside we will be hurt, but eventually we need to realise that it is not that others hurt us deliberately; it is we who have a predisposition to be hurt because we are inwardly attacking ourselves.

Being so sensitive, a Chiron person is able to see that everyone has areas like this. We see how people are imprisoned by damaging, negative thoughts about themselves, and we are able to say the very thing that helps to find the break in the wall. Focusing on them, we have taken attention away from our own wound; dealing with the same kind of pain in others, our perspective grows. This wound to the personality cannot be healed from outside because we are causing it ourselves, but it is very difficult to stop the damage without outside help or stimulus of some kind.

Chiron is in touch with the truth about people, and instinctively tells that truth. He is the truth-teller whose function is to help us be born into our potential. Wielding the truth, this cosmic midwife sets people free (Uranus) from the prison of their limiting beliefs (Saturn). People may, or may not, appreciate hearing the truth at the time; but consciously saying the right thing at the needed moment is healing of the highest order. We need to encourage people who have such accurate sensitivity, to tell the truth they know, and they need to learn to do it with love at the right time. Author Frederick Bailes in his book about positive thinking, called *Hidden Power for Human Problems*,[1] referred to the highest form of healing as 'waking someone from their dream'.

(Chiron's chart position shows where we lack confidence so debilitatingly, and learn that it is our own woundedness that hurts and not that others hurt us. This position will also indicate where we try to do the best to help or heal others and the form of healing that will flow most naturally for us and from us.)

[1] Bailes, F. Hidden Power for Human Problems, DeVorss, 1994.

The Planets - how they rule the Zodiac Signs

There are similarities between the vibration of a planet and the qualities of the particular Zodiac Sign it has been chosen to rule in traditional astrology. The outer expression of a planet is reflected in Signs which have qualities of Air and Fire, the lighter elements vibrating faster. Their inner expression is reflected in Signs which have qualities of Water and Earth, the heavier elements.

The Moon and Sun rule Cancer and Leo respectively. Moving from Cancer to Leo is like crossing the moment between night and day, like dawn. The other five planets of the original seven rule two Signs each. Between them, those two express the planet's inner and outer concerns. Saturn, the furthest of these from the Sun, rules the Signs of Capricorn and Aquarius, opposite the two 'lights', and is therefore said to be the 'Master of Darkness', darkness being our experience of the dense Earth.

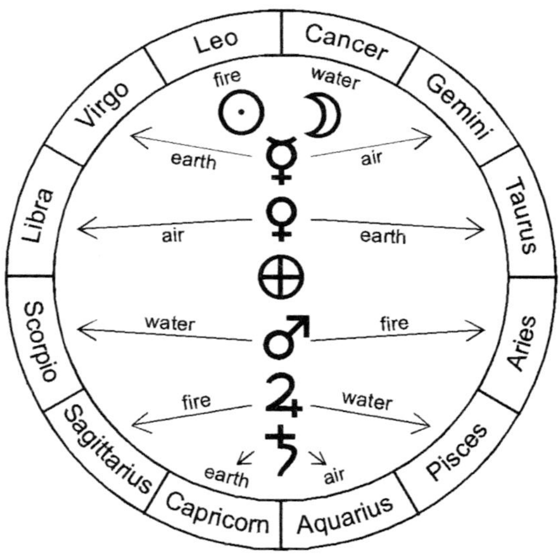

When a planet is travelling across, or transiting, the Sign it rules, its energy is increased. When it transits the Sign *opposite* the one that it rules, its energy is reduced. Some Sign qualities enhance, or 'Exalt', the energy of a planet, while the opposite Signs work against the energy to the planet's 'Detriment', then its positive expression is less easy. The following section focuses on the essential connections between the planets and their traditional Signs of Rulership. In the solar system as a whole, each individual planet, Sun, Moon and Earth, represents a part of that whole.

The Sun represents our essential self - spirit-fire. ☉
Its purpose is to remind us of the impulse towards creation, the point radiating from the centre of the circle, the heart of all our endeavours. It is the outer expression of the Light through the Zodiac.
(outer) **rules Leo** (Fire), expressing spirit-fire - radiating

The Moon represents our unconscious - reflector of universal spirit light to those in the 'night' of material, Earthly life. ☽
Its purpose is to bathe us in that light through experiencing the spectrum of the twelve moods of the Zodiac cycle. If we are working with full and new Moons, the Moon in relationship with the Sun, we would experience one Zodiac Sign each calendar month. If we are working with the movement of the Moon itself through the Zodiac we would experience all twelve Signs each 28 days, thirteen times a year. It is the inner expression of the Light through the Zodiac, balancing the Sun.
(inner) **rules Cancer** (Water), responsive to the moods of Nature - containing.

☿ **Mercury** represents our mind - conscious thought - knowledge - communication.
Its purpose is to carry the communications of the planets to each other and to the sun, so that they are not divided by their separate existence; and to interpret, and express the Light of the Sun through the mind.
(outer) **rules Gemini** (Air), seeking to know by looking and finding out - communicating discoveries brings understanding.
(inner) **rules Virgo** (Earth), seeking to know by experiment, seeks perfection through trying many ways - trying to improve order brings understanding.

♀ **Venus** represents the energy of attraction - relationship - love.
Its purpose is to counter the force that separates forms so that they should not lose touch with each other.
(outer) **rules Libra** (Air), mental harmony - diplomacy, discussion - love of humanity.
(inner) **rules Taurus** (Earth), physical harmony - security, beauty - love of Earth

⊕ **The Earth** is the nest where new forms are hatched - the womb of physical creation.
Its purpose is to feed its children abundantly.

♂ **Mars** represents the energy of will, motive force - the power-house.
Its purpose is to assert the expression of the solar system (our character) - to be effective.
(outer) **rules Aries** (Fire), drive to become separate - activity - will to express life.
(inner) **rules Scorpio** (Water), drive to control emotions -reservoir of energy - will to determine life.

Jupiter represents expansion - growth. ♃
Its purpose is to discover what is outside the system, so that the assertiveness of Mars will not destroy or damage the unknown.
(outer) **rules Sagittarius** (Fire), through interest - gift of attention - generosity in enthusiasm - philosopher.
(inner) **rules Pisces** (Water), through compassion - gift of the martyr (Jesus was sacrificed at the beginning of the Age of Pisces) - generosity in service - philanthropist.

Saturn represents structure - the laws of necessity. ♄
Its purpose is to limit the expansion of created forms so that their strength is not outgrown - to check that growth is durable and appropriate.
(outer) **rules Aquarius** (Air), in thought - social structure - laws - traditional behaviour secures society.
(inner) **rules Capricorn** (Earth), in the physical world - labour - work - well built foundation secures building.

The system of seven planets round the Earth lasted in Western thinking for thousands of years. As technology, and consequently astronomical understanding, increased, the outer planets were discovered, each discovery reflecting an aspect of growth in humanity at the time. Each planet was assigned to a Zodiac Sign, expanding the meaning of that Sign to include humanity's corresponding growth.

Uranus, discovered in 1781, reflected the new social mobility possible at the time of the industrial revolution, and also the beginnings of work with electricity. ♅
Uranus draws into **Aquarius** (Air) consciousness a freedom of movement, sudden surprising changes, a magical quality.

♆ **Neptune**, discovered in 1846, reflected a resurgence of spiritual activity for the masses, meditation and communication with the non-physical becoming accessible for the non-religious. Also photography was in its infancy, the ability to fake or gloss over reality.
Neptune draws into **Pisces** (Water) consciousness the psychic and emotional sensitivity, the mystical quality.

♇ **Pluto**, discovered in 1930, reflected the secret development of the H-bomb. When this finally exploded into public awareness in 1945, it set in motion an overturning of attitudes. This change was based on the realisation that humanity had the power to destroy itself and its world, so was no longer able to hide in the role of nature's victim.
Pluto draws into **Scorpio** (Water) consciousness the power to use the deepest emotions to rise to the heights of personal development, the transformative quality.

⚷ **Chiron**, discovered in 1977, reflects the rise in complementary and natural therapies and personal growth work as so many people, wounded on many levels, are finding ways to heal and be healed. We are realising that surviving through suppression, manipulation and control creates a prison which restricts our true potential. Through being in touch with, and understanding, the emotions locked into our systems during childhood, and also through being true to our own hearts, human beings become able to make the step towards more responsible care of themselves, of each other and of the Earth.

There is no overall agreement among astrologers as to which Sign is ruled by Chiron, but I favour the idea that it might be best ruling **Virgo** (an Earth Sign), because it draws into the consciousness of that Sign the focus on service and the healing power of the truth - the quality of a catalyst.

"Why the planets were formed"

an imaginative story

As part of my enquiry into the meanings within our solar system, I asked inside myself for a new way to express the idea of the planets. I found myself looking inwardly at what I already knew, but from a different perspective. Allowing a sense of creativity to find new words, this is what came to me:

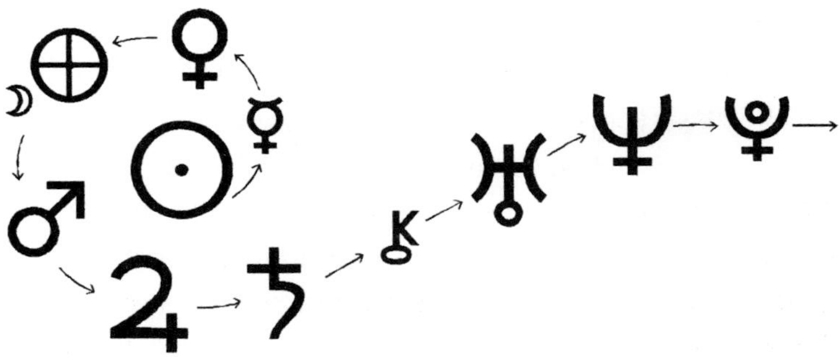

"In the beginning there was a Light space filled with potential." *(I saw a circle.)*

"The point of an idea arrived from the source of creation *(a dot arrived in the circle's centre)* and began to attract the stuff of manifestation. Where the point had been, there grew a brilliant light focusing all the Light that had been diffuse in space. You call that light, **the Sun**." ☉

"The original idea was now separate from the Light, and integrated the principle of separation into itself by dividing and dividing into an infinity of potential forms.

Each form also divided into ever increasing complexity and density, while the principles of their life were mirrored by the manifestation of the planets."

"Which planet came first?" I asked.

"**Mercury** ☿ manifested close to the Sun to express the idea of communication and interpretation of the Light. There had been no need for communication before the ideas, because all was One. But as the forms felt themselves separate one from another, there seemed to be a need for a link between them and Mercury is that link. That is why he is called 'the Messenger of the Gods'.

"**Venus** ♀ was the idea that, even though the forms were separate, they would not grow too far apart. Venus is the attracting force of love which prevents the planets from spinning off too far from each other.

"**Earth** ⊕ manifested as the nest where new forms are hatched on this imagined material level: the womb of physical creation. This womb closed in on itself, feeling the need to protect its young, and the **Moon** ☽ manifested to keep contact with the rest of the system. Rolling around its mother, the Moon expresses the qualities of each Zodiac Sign in turn, a clear channel to and from the cosmos.

"**Mars** ♂ is the principle of assertiveness so that all life on the planetary level shall be able to move about and express itself effectively. Combined with the protective urge, this principle can lead to attack for survival.

"**Jupiter** ♃ ensures that life will not express the growth of its forms without knowing how the rest of existence is reacting. Jupiter is the expansion outwards to find out about the rest of creation, so that the Martian expression does not destroy wantonly or unconsciously. Therefore it represents the 'higher' consciousness.

"**Saturn** ♄ is the beloved. Cold, fresh, keeping all this planetary growth from its own ignorant or inappropriate advance, Saturn stands guard over the nest, and teaches all beings grown here to be sufficiently in touch with their own truth so as to understand the rest of the cosmos when they actually make the connection.

"**Uranus** ♅ is wildness, shocking the nest from outside the confines of Saturn to make sure that the beings don't grow too complacent or too slowly within Saturn's care, for they could remain within the nest for the sake of security, or through fear of the unknown. From time to time Uranus sends out new visions of life's possibilities, using electrical excitement to tempt spirit out of the safety of its many separate identities in form.

"**Neptune** ♆ soothes the freed beings, humming in harmony with the cosmos, a dreamy sound that lulls them into a boundless state where communication with the cosmos becomes possible. Neptune is the principle of blending which culminates in merging with all that is, becoming One in the Great Unity.

"**Pluto** ♇ sets the scene for change, and makes the transformation from planetary identity to cosmic vision for any being that appears ready, and has agreed with the cosmos to accept spirit in place of form."

"What about **Chiron** ⚷ ?" I asked. "Was a maverick thrown into this system to stir things up?"

"Yes, Chiron is not the first and it will not be the last, but it is the relevant one for this time of your growth. Chiron's job is to wake you to your next steps, so that you will see that those steps are for your own healing and not just a whim of the cosmos.

It is time to grow into another realm of greatness, still tiny in the whole of things but realising your many levels of possible awareness and even expanding you backwards/forwards into the stuff of which you were first formed, the great Unity. Chiron is the guide that lifts your feet firmly one at a time and moves them forward in growth. A careful teacher during a painful process but you will not need it for long.

"This whole pattern of planets is yourself. It is not separate. And each planet, like each chakra, reflects an entire dimension of being to which you become open and conscious if you tune into that planet to contact its principle. Please do tune in. You will be assisting your growth as an individual. You will grow a greater understanding of yourself and life by expanding your consciousness in this way!"

This is a story.
It shows the unfolding principles
of the life we know.

Exercise:

Spend a little time sitting quietly with eyes closed, pondering on one of the planets, or the Sun or Moon. Ask inside yourself for a greater understanding of the principle that your chosen planet exemplifies. Relax your body, open your mind, and allow ideas to flow without hindering or checking them.

Afterwards, do make a note of what happened. Sometimes the full meaning takes a while to arrive.

The Planets

Part 2

Ways in which we are different

In everybody's chart you will find all the same planets and all the same Signs; we know that all the principles apply to everyone. The difference between one chart and another is that each planet could be in any one of twelve different Zodiac Signs, and these qualify, or colour, the energy of that planetary principle. The Sign a planet occupies indicates *the style of behaviour* that we tend to use when involved in activities requiring that planetary energy or function.

When we meet another person using one of their planetary energies in the same Sign, we see that same style of behaviour and we recognise it as natural and feel at home with that person, at least in that part of our own nature. Comparing charts can be fascinating and very useful in relationships. Chart comparison, as a branch of natal astrology, is called Synastry.

Each planet will also be in one of twelve Houses, showing which activities or people in our life trigger the energy flow. In this chapter I shall be looking at only the planets in Zodiac Signs, but considering the Houses also would, of course, give much more personal information.

One way of looking at the seven chakra-based planets is to think of the Zodiac Sign through which the planet is moving as a doorway to that chakra in the body, so each of the chakras would have a Zodiac Sign over its opening. It is easiest if the doorway is suitable for the energy that needs to come through. Sometimes, however, the *quality* of the doorway is less conducive to a free flow of energy. In this case, a few adjustments to personal expectations would help to get the best results.

For instance: in this system of correspondences Mars relates to the solar plexus chakra. If Mars was moving through Aries at the time of birth, the function of solar plexus energy will be flowing out through an Aries doorway: drive and assertiveness will be of an Aries style - the person in action will be fast, direct, clear.

On the other hand, if Mars was moving through Pisces, the function of solar plexus energy will be flowing out through a Pisces doorway: drive and assertiveness will be of a Piscean style - the person in action will be gentle, tentative, easily influenced. The Aries way is more traditionally expected from the solar plexus: Mars is said to rule Aries. The Pisces way does not make asserting oneself easy unless one is looking at situations and people that require very sensitive handling, where the Aries Mars would be likely to upset people by being too brusque.

Mars in Pisces may not assert itself in the direct way we traditionally expect, but it definitely has its virtues in a situation requiring empathy, and the person who has it needs to know this in order to feel that their way is acceptable, so they can accept themselves as they are.

The energy flowing freely through each of the chakras creates health in that chakra at all levels of vibration, so that we have access to the physical, vital and emotional levels and so on right through to Source. When we give ourselves what we need to be healthy and happy, the Zodiac doorways of the chakras will be open and we will be radiating the qualities of the different Signs represented. The more healthy and open our system, the better able we are to express spirit on Earth, which has a knock-on effect on those around us, and is ultimately what helps other people best.

The relationship of planets to each other - called 'Aspects'

Every part of a birth chart can be interpreted in a negative way or a positive way, including the relationships between the planets. Some of those relationships, or 'aspects', seem to reflect impossibly difficult and painful experiences, and yet what we learn through them can become the source of our greatest strength and a gift to the rest of the world.

Also, each planetary relationship indicates a talent with which we were born, but most talents have to be developed through working them; very few are completely automatic. So it is that *every* aspect has its virtues, but also its drawbacks when used unconsciously. It is the personality of a person that is bothered by 'difficult' aspects, not their spirit.

An 'aspect' is the geometrical relationship between any two points in the Zodiac, as a proportion of the 360° of a circle, giving us the major shapes of a hexagon (sextile), a square (square), a triangle (trine) and the line division into duality (opposition). The aspects that are normally taken into account are multiples of 30 degrees as these have been found to be most indicative of noticeable character traits. Most of these are referred to as Major Aspects, but they include one so-called Minor Aspect, the Quincunx of 150°.

As the aspects show an energy relationship between two planets, we can start to consider the quality of that energy by putting one end in Aries, the Sign of outward energy expression. Then we will be able to derive some of the qualities of the aspect from the Signs which hold its other end.

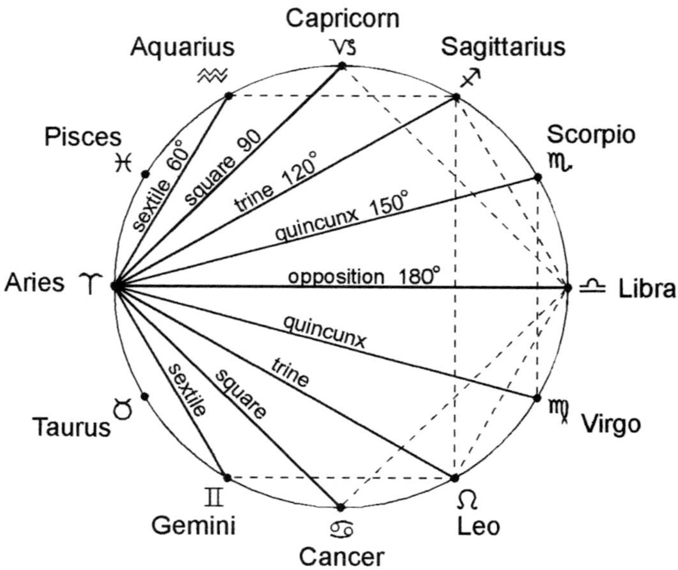

Any major aspect, as listed below, indicates that the two planets are significantly connected and therefore due to work together as two facets of character that are always triggered into action at the same time. Each planet can be visualised as an independent character on a stage in the 'play' of your life by blending the energy of the planet with the quality of the Sign it occupies, and imagining a person with that character being concerned with the things of that House. The specific aspect shows whether the two characters find that working together comes easily or whether it requires effort to get the best out of the combination.

The characters may not like each other at first, not understanding what the other is about, but we can imagine them learning to appreciate each other's finer qualities, and eventually even working together on the same job. Often a combination which starts as a problem, becomes a special power or talent as the person owning the chart gets to know themselves and redirects the energy. Sometimes a person is not prepared to put in that effort, and the difficulty can remain for this entire lifetime.

The major aspects are multiples of 30 degrees. Astrologers traditionally allow a number of degrees either side of an exact aspect, and the characteristic will be less pronounced the further the aspect is out of exactness. I always draw lines on a chart between planets in aspect to each other, and I personally use a colour code so that I can see at a glance what the relationship between them is like. I give the colours here in brackets. The descriptions of the particular relationships are given next, and they are followed by a list 'in brief' for easy reference on page 113.

A **conjunction** *(yellow)* is two or more planets occupying the same position in the Zodiac and working as one. They cannot work independently of each other although they may take turns in being the more powerful of the group. This tends to show in a person as an intense reaction to the area of life shown by the planets' position, and it will be more complex and strenuous when the two straddle the point between two Signs, because then the elements they are functioning through will not be in natural harmony; Fire or Air with Water or Earth.. ☌

A **sextile** *(green line)* is 60° between two planets (two Signs between them or a sixth of the circle), and shows constructive use of the planetary energies in harmony with each other. It tends to show in a person as an ability or strength of character. The Signs involved will tend to be complementary elements, Earth and Water, or Air and Fire, and lend the support of their different qualities to each other. ⚹

A **square** *(red line)* is 90° between two planets (three Signs between them or a quarter of the circle), and the planetary energies will each be expressing themselves very □

differently due to being in inharmonious elements. Because their styles of expression are so different, they tend not to understand each other, so there is often a conflict between them. It tends to show in a person as completely contradictory attitudes or behaviour at different times and a blind spot between them so that the person is unaware of the contradiction.

This results in arguments with the outside world, as one energy tends to be projected onto other people or situations while the person expresses the other. At some point there will be an inner flip, and the argument will be the other way around. If and when the person admits that the conflict is within them, the aspect can become an energy source.

Knowledge of the birth chart can be used to facilitate this in two ways: firstly, by imagining the planets in their Signs as characters on a stage and working out in an objective way how they can be brought to an acceptance of each other; secondly, by working out, and getting involved in, an activity that would use both energies at the same time.

△ A **trine** *(blue line)* is 120° between two planets (four Signs between them or one third of the circle). They will usually be in the same element, which allows for such an easy flow between them that they work together without the person realising. This tends to show as an easy talent or skill which the person takes for granted in themselves, and they may assume other people have the same ability. The risk is that other people are seen as stupid or lazy because they do not act with the same skill.

Because the skill tends to be unconscious, depending which planets are involved, it can operate as a weakness which only becomes strength as the confidence is achieved to handle it in the world. Empathy with others can feel like being too sensitive, and a strong sense of responsibility can be a lonely burden when a person feels they must keep shouldering more. Once we are conscious of having this special skill, we can take more care to use it wisely when necessary and conserve, rather than waste, our energy.

A **quincunx** *(brown line)* is 150° between two planets ⚻ (five Signs between them. Two quincunxes plus a sextile create a shape called 'yod' or 'finger of God' .) It is referred to as a minor aspect because the characteristics only show when it is fairly exact, say between 148° and 152° apart. The planetary energies will be in inharmonious elements and tend at first to weaken and undermine each other's full functioning.

It can feel like an energy drain due to negative assumptions, like "no-one will understand me, so why bother to explain", or "I'll never succeed, why try!" There is a tendency to expect to gain personal comfort and happiness from outside ourselves, and we consistently undermine our efforts to do that. Not fulfilling our own needs weakens our effectiveness.

Those who have denied their own needs have to break through their guilt feelings to spend time nurturing themselves, rather than just hoping others will do it for them. Nurturing ourselves first gives us the health and vitality we need in order to serve others well. Then, when this person chooses to help others, they discover the joy of service and then all the love and support they craved before comes to them naturally.

It is important not to sacrifice anything of oneself supposedly for another. Service needs to be a natural giving of one's energy from an inner abundance. Any other giving has a sense of need as its source and consequently is of no real help to anyone. A quincunx seems to be like a fail-safe mechanism that a spirit includes in its personality when it is determined to remember why it came into earth: when this personality focuses exclusively on personal comfort, the person is unhappy, but when they turn outwards to love and help others - fulfilling the spirit's purpose - the world gives them all they desired in the first place. The special service this person has to give will be shown by the planetary virtues that are quincunx to each other.

☍ An **opposition** *(mauve line)* is 180° between two planets (six Signs between them or half the circle). These planets work in directions which are opposite but generally in complementary elements. It tends to feel like an inner tussle which the person is aware of, like an argument they keep having with themselves, and it may show in them as uncertainty or vacillation of attitude. The awareness the person has of their difficulty brings a measure of consciousness of self, a valuable quality which is essential for inner growth and development.

I do not use other **minor aspects** because I find the above aspects sufficient to do the work for which I am suited, and I like the simplicity. Apart from the semi-sextile (exactly 30° - two planets that do not work together), they are not multiples of 30°, which is the limit I have chosen for my work. They are valid and provide information, but to keep things simple I will not go into them here.

A list of Aspects in Brief

(with suggestions for working with them in a birth chart)

☌ **Conjunction** *(circled with yellow)* up to 5° or even 8° apart. Two or more planets in the same place in the Zodiac - cannot work independently. In a character it will be an intensity in that area which is described by the combination of both planets.

Exercise: In a specific chart, think about how the two principles involved would blend.

⚹ **Sextile** *(green line)* 2 Signs or 60° apart + or - 5°. Two planetary principles working constructively together - strengthening the character.

Exercise: In a specific chart, think about how the particular planets would help each other.

□ **Square** *(red line)* 3 Signs or 90° apart + or - 8°. Here two planets challenge each other with conflicting methods or styles causing an unconscious vacillation of behaviour between the two. When working for the same purpose consciously, the planets create a powerful ability.

Exercise: In a specific chart, think about the planets as characters on a stage and how you would get them to work together. What single job would you give them to bring out the best qualities of both?

△ **Trine** *(blue line)* 4 Signs or 120° + or - 8°. There is an easy flow between these planets indicating a talent or skill which tends to be taken for granted and is therefore expected in others. The skill is a blend of both planetary energies in the Signs and Houses they occupy.

Exercise: In a specific chart, think about how the skill could be used in a satisfying and valuable way.

⚻ **Quincunx** *(brown line)* 5 Signs or 150° + or - 2°.
Two planets that tend to undermine and weaken each other. Negative assumptions can act like an energy drain, preventing action. The planets work well together when used for others, and the aspect then shows a special ability.

Exercise: In a specific chart, think about what the undermining thoughts or feelings might be, and what special area of service might be indicated by the blending of the qualities of both energies plus Signs and Houses occupied.

☍ **Opposition** *(mauve line)* 6 Signs or 180° + or - 8°.
Two planets that create tension by holding opposing viewpoints simultaneously. The consequent inner argument brings valuable self-awareness.

Exercise: In a specific chart, think about how each viewpoint tends to balance the other.

Conjunctions, Squares, Quincunxes or Oppositions are said to be challenging or conflicting aspects, while Sextiles or Trines are said to be supporting or flowing aspects. It is important to remember, however, that the particular planets involved and also their Sign and House positions may alter these generalisations.

The Seven Chakra Planets in a birth chart: Signs and Aspects

There follow some examples of planets in Zodiac Signs, in aspect to each other, to show how the astrological information can be used. The exercises listed after each planet can be carried out by anyone, but those who have a printout of their birth chart, or even a list of the Zodiac positions of their planets, will be able to apply more of what is given.

Our essential character

☉

Heart centre, **Sun** *(green) - consciousness of essential Self, or spirit, for understanding and love*

Your **Sun** Sign is the way to "be yourself" so that your heart can be open. We need to be expressing ourselves from that heart-Sign in order to feel centred. Only in that state can we accept our personality. Without the energy through the heart, the personality cannot understand what is going on in life. It feels as though the light is out, every problem is like another hurdle in a pointless obstacle race. When the sun is shining and the Sun-Sign apparent in our radiation, each new problem is simply what we are doing, no big deal! Chapter 2 on Zodiac Signs (Part 2) speaks of this essential character, explaining how each of the Signs behaves the way they do because of how they feel. If we know how they feel, we can understand their behaviour and understanding allows for tolerance.

In some birth charts the Sun makes no connections with other planets, it is 'unaspected'. This shows a person who feels themselves to be tucked away inside, not actually making deep contact with other people through operating their personality. This is because their personality, reflected by the planets, is not in contact with their spirit through the heart, rather like the image of a wheel where there are no spokes between the hub and the rim. It can feel a bit lonely, and there is a difficulty in locating a sense of commitment to most activities, but if that person will spend time creating an inner relationship, getting to know themselves inside, they will be creating 'spokes' for the wheel. They will find a wealth of strength and joy like a reservoir, and expressing that to others is something that improves throughout their life.

Any aspects the Sun makes to other planets indicates that those are qualities we are integrating into our central character, difficult aspects indicating that issues around those planets' Signs and Houses have to be worked out or cleared in the process.

Meditation Exercise:

When sitting quietly, close your eyes and feel your breathing opening and collapsing your chest. Become aware that your heart is in the middle, being massaged by the breath.

A vision that is wonderful for anyone, but particularly appropriate for Fire Signs, Aries, Leo and Sagittarius, is a closed lotus or water-lily type flower with thousands of petals, at your heart centre in the middle of your chest cavity. With each breath allow some of those petals to open. Hidden in the centre of the flower is a light, and as the petals gradually open it can be seen shining through a little brighter. With every breath more petals open, the light shines more brightly still. Keep going as long as you wish, there need be no end to the number of petals, and allow the light that shines to permeate your whole being and all the space around you.

Another vision for the breath, more appropriate for Air Signs, Gemini, Libra and Aquarius, is the image of a bird. You are that bird flying in slow motion; as you breathe in, your wings rise and as you breathe out they lower. Fly wherever you wish and for as long as you like.

A peaceful meditation for Water Signs, Cancer, Scorpio and Pisces, is the sea. In this case the breath becomes the waves on the shore, the in-breath as the sea draws back and the out-breath as the wave lazily breaks on the shore.

For Earth Signs, Taurus, Virgo and Capricorn, it would be more appropriate to feel yourself as a tree using your breathing to draw life up from the Earth, and extend your branches, twigs and leaves into the cosmos. Later, or concurrently, draw light down from the cosmos into your crown chakra, and send it into the Mother Earth through your roots. Feel for the sensation of the Earth's own heartbeat while letting your breathing slow down, and allow a deep sense of Oneness with nature to develop.

Our personal unconscious

Crown centre, ***Moon*** *(amethyst) - energy of universal spirit for responding and playing with creation*

Moon is our personal unconscious, which includes our assumptions and expectations about life, our prejudices, instinctive behaviour and the habitual emotional reactions we survived with as children. Projection onto our world is largely unconscious, and so it is the Moon that shows much of what we see coming back to us from our world. Here we are very sensitive and feel the aspects to the Moon acutely, wincing with the difficulties, relaxing with help and approval. This is where we know what hurts us and what is nurturing to us and we can help ourselves if we listen to it.

We can connect with this side of ourselves through our dreams and our emotional moods.

We are expressing our instinctive reactions most of the time, especially in long term relationships. It is difficult to remain conscious and aware of our responses at all times, and relationships often fall gradually into a list of habit patterns. Habits are governed by the Moon, so when comparing charts of people living together, it is important that each person be aware of the relationship between their own Moon and the other person's birth chart. If there are appreciative connections, supportive aspects, they will be able to rub along together relatively comfortably even in unconscious mode. If there are conflicting connections, the habits of one will grate on the other and they will need to be more aware of how they are behaving.

If both people in such a relationship are working on growth as individuals, they will approach the problem with a desire to become more aware. With the determination to be honest about how they feel, and the acceptance that the partner is a reflection of our own unconscious patterns, the relationship can flourish. Otherwise, they will upset each other unintentionally so often, they may not be able to work through the distress.

Aspects to the Moon indicate planetary energies that are affected by our unconsciousness all the time. When the aspects are conflicting, they are prone to being projected; we tend to blame other people for any difficulties. When flowing aspects link planets to the Moon, the indication is of open acceptance of those principles from
☽♋ birth; Moon in Cancer will accept them unquestioningly,
☽♐ Moon in Sagittarius may well question but still receives the impressions.

As Moon is the principle of mothering, all connections to the Moon may show something of how we perceived mother in childhood. It is important to remember that she will actually have had many attributes, and also that the child's perceptions are set before birth.

Locating painful childhood experiences is a part of many development processes because our early treatment, traumas and circumstances seem to set the pattern for much of our inappropriate adult behaviour. But the clue to a healthy energy flow through the crown chakra is the Moon-Sign at its *happiest*, because happiness prevents any darkness from increasing and also dissolves many of the blockages.

Even in an unhappy childhood there will be experiences that indicate the way in which this child could have been happy, spontaneous and natural, however brief those moments might be. When we remember the feeling of those moments, we are better able to let go of the negative emotional reactions that block the crown chakra. Some aspects of our child-state are shown by the Moon-Sign in our birth chart, such as the kind of thing you need in order to feel secure. The position of the Moon will show many things that went wrong for you as a child, but the Sign itself will also indicate what activities would have pleased you.

The trick in adult life is to go for doing the Moon-Sign activity for the fun of it, not for gain. As children, what we wanted to do was enjoy ourselves but there are twelve different qualities of activity that may create that enjoyment.

A person with Moon in Leo might have enjoyed ☽♌
being a star, dressing up or performing in front of an approving audience. They may not have had enough approval and love to dare to do these things, but knowing that this field would have pleased them, they can now go for that field as an adult and bring out the child with joy through leading children's play, amateur dramatics or other out front playful activities.

☽ ♍ If the Moon was in Virgo, the activities would be completely different. Here one would need to look at organizing something carefully for the fun of it, sorting out a mess, doing a great job of organizing one's accounts, making fiddly things as presents, organizing charity work, mending things, or simply enjoying being able to help people.

☽ ♋ Moon in Cancer's field would be more in the line of playing at parenting. As an adult, a Cancer Moon would need to be careful not to be too weighed down by responsibility, and the best activity would be parenting themselves, pampering themselves rather than hoping that someone else will do it.

☽ ♑ A Capricorn Moon-child on the other hand, would enjoy taking responsibility to a degree, but not the kind of overloading by parents or a difficult home situation that may have occurred in childhood. Perhaps the adult would enjoy to be involved in voluntary countryside care, like clearing footpaths or building bridges over streams, dressmaking or making toys or furniture.

Exercise:

So, find an activity that you would enjoy that expresses the Sign of the Moon in your chart, and make it a non-paying hobby. You will discover that the child within is still ready to play and you will become happier and more creative as a result.

Exercise:

Using an experience that keeps cropping up as a reflection, see if you can discover in yourself an attitude or feeling of which you were previously unaware.

Our mind

Brow centre, ***Mercury*** *(indigo) - mental energy for vision and communication*

Mercury is meant to be an awareness in the spaces between the thousand thoughts that cloud our mind, because this is where we get the inspiration to understand the truth of the present moment by being fully present. Mercury is where we can consciously work to free ourselves from our mistaken views, as we learn to control our thinking. In practice Mercury represents what we are conscious of most of the time, what preoccupies us. These thoughts are generally of the past and the future which can be affected by us only through our attitude to them.

If Mercury is in an Earth Sign, you will notice practical things most. If it is in a Water Sign, you will be more aware of emotions, yours and other people's; your thinking will be coloured by emotional states and issues, so it would be wise not to make decisions while feeling depressed or worried, because they will limit you when you are feeling better. If it is in an Air Sign, Mercury's natural element of ideas, your mind will be consciously active mostly with words, ideas and conversations. If Mercury is in a Fire Sign, you will be focused on imaginative solutions, visions of possibilities, lateral thinking, seeing the positive side.

The level of experience you naturally focus on indicates the kind of problems you have, because it is our thinking that makes something a problem rather than the thing itself. To someone else, our problems may be no problem at all!

For example: Mercury in Pisces, having no natural boundaries, will overlap the minds of everyone around. They will be constantly aware of how other people are feeling and in order to feel emotionally good themselves, they will feel the need to create everyone else feeling good too. So they tend to get involved in sorting out other people's problems instead of focusing on, and sorting out, their own life. A Piscean way of getting to the central point of clarity, would be asking for guidance from the Light in meditation where the overlap will be with wiser aspects of themselves and the Light companionship.

☿♎ Mercury in Libra indicates a focus on relationship, a person who is always trying to keep the peace, find the harmonious thing to say or at least a pleasant way of saying whatever it is. This person will tend to always have at least one relationship that they feel is in difficulty and that will be their preoccupying thought. A Libran way of getting to the central point of balance, would be to step back and contemplate the relationship from the point of view of a benevolent judge, listening to all sides and allowing the correct path to become clear.

Supportive, flowing aspects to Mercury indicate aspects of the personality that we can tune into consciously, and that we use when we talk with people. Conflicting aspects show the same potential, but we have to be flexible enough to realize that what is being reflected to us from the world is that conflicting energy. Once the connection has been made, this conscious ability will be powerful.

We need to remember that we are busily creating all our experience; firstly by expecting things to be a certain way before they happen, waiting for people to behave the way we expect them to, and so on. Secondly, we interpret whatever happens in our own special way depending on what experience we have had before. Twelve people, each with Mercury in different Signs, will each have their own priorities and assumptions. Every person tends to think that other people's priorities and assumptions are the same as their own. So a person's reactions to what you say to them may well be unrelated to what you intended. They are not being obtuse, they are not necessarily deliberately attacking you, or misunderstanding you on a personal level. They are probably reacting to what they would have meant if they had said what you said. People's reactions tell you about them.

Exercise:

Try stepping back from your latest problem and look at the judgments you are making about the situation. Imagine how it would look if your Mercury was in a different Element from where it is. For instance, the emotional aspect of a situation that is worrying the Water Mercury, may be slight and passing compared with the physical security that the situation offers Earth, or the fun there can be in it for Fire. This will help you to see the situation in the round, to get it all in perspective.

Exercise:

If you have a specific problem, pause your thoughts for just a moment. Notice what surrounds you, all that your senses can tell you. Relax just for a moment, lifting your awareness from stomach, chest or mouth, wherever you keep it, into the centre of your head, projecting forward through that central window just above the eyebrow line.

Then define your problem so that your Higher Self can see it from the personality point of view and, if you find that you really want to solve it, ask for help. At the moment you ask for help, you need to decide to *listen* in silence within yourself for whatever it takes to bring about the solution and, once you know what it's going to take, carry that out. This exercise helps to clear away our preoccupations so that we can be more in touch with the moment we are in.

♀ Our personal love

Throat centre, ***Venus*** *(sky blue) - attracting energy for balancing and relating*

Venus represents the way we recognise and express appreciation and love. It is the way we express ourselves in relationship, what we radiate to people, our tastes, how our feminine side feels.

The danger at the throat chakra is the vacuum that opens out when we long for love that never seems to come. What we are doing is projecting that absence of love into our atmosphere, so we will see only needy people to relate to. The solution is to get the energy flowing out from us instead of trying to suck it in, and to do that we need to create the Venus Sign energy for ourselves. This will give us the feeling of love inside, and from there the love we give out will reflect love back to us from others. Unless one is in the place of love inside, it is impossible to feel it, whether it is coming from outside or not.

♀♉ A Taurus Venus needs to appreciate their body and demonstrate that appreciation by giving comfort and love through food that is tasty but also healthy, and through exercise out in nature. Dressing in sensual materials, receiving massage, always asking the body what will feel comfortable, any of these things will give the whole person a sense of being loved.

♀♊ Venus in Gemini, relating through words and communication, needs to talk with themselves, an inner conversation which may well result in writing - stories, articles, letters to friends. In this way they will be able to quietly tap into the imaginative side of the brain and the whole experience will feel more fulfilling than talking only with others. Fulfilling themselves mentally will give this person the feeling of being loved and appreciated.

A feeling that often assails the throat area is what we call 'a lump in the throat', when we are experiencing an emotion that we feel we cannot let out properly in the situation. As Venus is about love and relatedness, we can help that lump of energy to disperse by looking to see how other people are feeling and giving some loving concern to someone else.

Venus represents what we feel comfortable with, like to have around us, while Mars represents how we go about getting that. If Mars and Venus are at odds with each other in the birth chart, perhaps by Sign or by Squaring each other, then we will tend to try to get what we want in ways that push it away.

♀/♂

Venus in Gemini likes to relate through chatting and a Mars Square to it in Virgo is likely to be so concerned with being accurate that the talking becomes stilted and everybody feels inhibited.

Venus in Taurus likes physical comfort and cuddling, while in the same chart Mars in Aquarius gets into intellectual arguments and the energy holds people at arm's length.

Once we know the qualities of these two, we will be clearer as to whether we really want the Venus qualities, and we have the option of choosing ways to behave that will achieve what we want.

One of the most important things we can understand from the placement of Venus in the chart is which of the twelve Zodiac styles of behaviour we recognise as loving. Venus in our chart is our manner of relating, and expressing appreciation and love to other people, especially our partners. The way other people express love to us will be in the style of their Venus by Sign and House.

♀ ♉ ♊

For instance, Venus in Gemini will express love by having a chat with the loved one. Venus in Taurus will express love by giving a hug or rubbing the shoulder of the

♀
♋ ♍

loved one. Venus in Virgo will help the loved one sort things out to show their love. Venus in Cancer will make a cup of tea to express their love. As this is the way they express love, it is also the way they recognise love coming to them from us.

If your Venus is in a different Sign from that of your partner's Venus you will probably be expressing your love in a different way from them. When the Signs are in inharmonious elements, it is very likely that you will not recognise the love in what your partner does for you. The result can be that both partners feel that they are giving love and not getting it back. The solution is to find the Sign of your partner's Venus and do for them what that Venus would do.

So often we give love in the way we want to receive it. So if you don't know a person's Venus Sign, just do for them what you see them do for the people they love. The Venus Sign is just the astrological clue to what the other person sees as love. One word of warning: don't give love in their style all the time because they will become dependent on you for that loved feeling and not get around to doing it for themselves.

Exercise:

Try to pick out the way a friend expresses their affection and ask if they feel more loved when others treat them that way. Check it in yourself as well.

Exercise:

While relating to family or friends, practice thinking "Who is this person really?" and let your impressions open your mind about them.

Our reservoir of emotional energy

Solar plexus, ***Mars*** *(yellow) - emotional energy for effective action and control*

Mars represents our energy for action, for getting what we want. The Sign Mars is in indicates the way we assert ourselves, how we deal with things, how we apply ourselves, and how our masculine side feels. An Aries Mars acts directly, fast, quite differently from a Pisces Mars which is sensitive, unsure; and there are another ten different styles.

A man with a Piscean or Cancer Mars will be an emotional, sensitive *man*. However, he may still have an abrupt way of relating if his Venus is in Aries; he may be unable to express the emotion in words if his Mercury is in Aquarius, a Sign which prefers not to own up to emotions at all, or if Mercury is Square to the Mars from Sagittarius which veers into looking for positive meaning rather than exploring the painful bits. On the other hand, a woman who has Mars in Pisces, while having an emotional, sensitive energy herself, will tend to be attracted to those qualities in a man.

Venus is the feminine identity and Mars is the masculine identity. When we relate to a person of the opposite sex, we tend to identify with the planet of our own sex and therefore project the other planet on that person. A woman will tend to identify with her Venus, however self-aware she is, when she is relating to a man. She will then naturally project her Mars onto him, so she will feel more drawn to him if he is like the Sign of Mars in her chart. Where he turns out to be different from that Mars, she may well feel that he is letting her down, that he no longer fits her, and the relationship will lose some of its original pull. All this is very unconscious. When she becomes aware of how she normally expresses her own Mars qualities, and chooses to express that energy as well as her feminine Venus energy in the relationship, she will be able to begin to see the man for who he really is, and true relating can start.

A man, similarly, projects his Venus onto the woman he relates to and, if he expects her to be the one who makes friends and concerns herself with the loving, while he acts out whatever masculine role his Mars Sign and House defines, he is likely to try and control her to behave like the Venus in his chart. When he concerns himself with loving in the relationship he will be expressing his own Venus and he will begin to be able to see her for who she really is.

Polarising into Mars or Venus can also happen between people of the same sex, where one of them has one of the two planets stronger in their chart than the other planet and so polarises into it in all relating situations. The result is that one can lose contact with one's Sun-Sign, one's central self; the personality is in complete control. The other effect of projecting one planet is a sense of being only half one's personality. Both effects can develop into dependence on the other person which is unhealthy for both people.

If the projected planet was one that we have difficulty expressing, or represents behaviour we reject in ourselves, projecting it onto someone else means that we will have difficulty with *them*. Accepting that those projected qualities are actually our own, not only enables us to see the other person more clearly, but also allows us to get on with them better.

Whatever its style, we all need to have the Mars energy flowing if we are to have the energy we need to accomplish our desires. Knowing the Mars Sign shows the kind of activity that will get us moving, start the engine. So when there is something that needs to be done and the energy is not there, a short time occupied with the activity of Mars Sign (and House) will turn the ignition, and once running we can drive it where we wish. Mars in Gemini,

Libra or Aquarius (Air Signs) tends to get going after a conversation with someone. Knowing this, when a task is to be done, they could begin by phoning a friend about it for five minutes and then use the energy aroused to do the job.

We all need Mars energy for working life, so it helps to choose a job that includes an aspect of that Sign. Energy for a Sagittarius Mars gets a kick-start from planning and considering greater possibilities, so the best kind of work would incorporate travel or stretching ideas beyond normal boundaries. Even though a person with Mercury in Gemini may have a preference for communicating, if they have Mars in Taurus, they will need some form of physical work in the job to trigger the necessary energy.

At the solar plexus, Mars centre, energy can also be lost, seeming to drain away. Some people are particularly prone to that feeling: those with Mars in a Water Sign (Cancer or Pisces particularly) or with connections to Neptune, are likely to find their energy disappearing when worrying about someone or something. Negative emotion uses our energy whether we are conscious of it or not, so that we feel exhausted without having done anything that appears to warrant it.

Mars in Aquarius on the other hand seems to be in command of their emotions but sometimes that is because they are not looking at them. Above the solar plexus is the diaphragm and Mars in both Aquarius and Scorpio (Fixed Signs) can hold the muscles involved quite rigid, thereby preventing the sensation of the emotions reaching the upper body where they keep their awareness. It is important for us all to know how we are feeling at the Mars centre because that is the truth of our emotional life, and if we don't know what is there, how can we be honest with others?

Exercise:

While being quiet with yourself, put your attention in your solar plexus and ask if there is anything it wishes to say to you. You can use the chart placing of your Mars to give you clues as to the kind of issue that might need to be examined.

Exercise:

When there is something you want to achieve, check out what in that achievement will inspire the driving motivation of your Mars Sign. Then practice deliberately invoking the energy at the Mars centre by focusing on that aspect of the task. As the energy wakes, use it to power your original desire into an intention. Emotional energy is one step nearer than thought to the vibration of the material world, and brings ideas further into manifestation.

2 Our growth

*Sexual centre, **Jupiter** (orange) - expansive energy for growth and compassion*

Jupiter represents our growth as individuals and our expansion in the world. The energy is triggered by pleasure in life. Whether enjoying ourselves physically, emotionally, mentally or spiritually, we reach out beyond what is necessary, setting in motion the creative flow of giving and receiving. We reach out on the physical level through bodily contact or sound or movement, on the emotional level through sympathy, feeling for someone else's experience. On the mental level we extend interest, and on the spiritual level, compassion. Because we are operating without fear at those times, we find ourselves doing things in new ways and finding creative solutions, revealing those potential gifts that others may have suspected in us but we were afraid to admit to.

The Jupiter Sign shows the kind of encouragement we need to stretch out and grow, and also the way in which we encourage others. Support, interest and acceptance need to be received in order to be given out to others, but we allow ourselves to receive them only if we have confidence that we deserve them. Without that sense of deserving, we cannot recognise encouragement when it is given.

For those of us whose old expectations of rejection or criticism created a childhood without acceptance and encouragement, there is a need to develop an acceptance and love of ourself, to give ourselves permission to be as we are, rather than constantly trying to be what we think others will approve. When we give ourselves permission to enjoy the Sign (and House) of Jupiter, one way or another other people will benefit from the flow. Everybody enjoys the energy of Jupiter, he is the beneficent 'father of the gods' creating a sense of abundant possibilities.

A person with Capricorn Jupiter will be expansive in practical ways. They enjoy developing a growing business or making plans for moving to a better home. They will be generous with advice about practical arrangements, and ready to take responsibility for situations that they create. They will always be ready to do what is necessary, with good feeling; a colleague who is a pleasure to work with. ♃♑

Jupiter in Aries would seem to be the antithesis of generosity because Aries is traditionally so self-involved, but as a child their confidence grows if allowed to be independent when they are ready, allowed to do things their own way, rather than having to be obedient or being ♃♈

rejected to manage on their own before they are competent. When they are able to enjoy having their own autonomy, they will encourage other people to be themselves and do their own thing; they will inspire courage by example.

♃♋

Jupiter in Cancer, on the other hand, feels the need of mothering care, emotional support. The emotional neediness of these people could easily hold back their growth, and they need to learn to give themselves gentle support and nurturing, so that they have within themselves enough to give from. Their way of encouraging others is to give them that support. They enjoy providing a home for those in need and being solicitous of other's feelings.

When Jupiter aspects another planet in a birth chart, it always increases whatever energy and activity that planet represents in its Sign and House, showing that Jupiter's own Sign and House are working for the other.

♃☍

When the aspect is an Opposition, Jupiter tends to have over-high expectations of the performance of the other planet, while if the aspect is a Square, the generosity of Jupiter is right over the top, reflecting a tendency to overdo the activity represented by the other planet until there is a need to retreat and recover, and the activity stops altogether for a while.

♃□

♃□♂

Jupiter Square Mars shows a tendency to feel over-optimistic about what one can achieve. Not allowing for limitations, the effort is put in to master the situation until the energy runs out and the person withdraws completely, feeling apathy or illness, or anger at their inability. This can clearly be remedied as the person learns to pace themselves. It is very important wherever Jupiter is in the chart, to be active in that area of life because that is where the enjoyment lies that will unlock our potential.

Jupiter energy is for us to grow, to unfold into all that we can be. There are two pitfalls we need to resist. One is the tendency to give it all to other people hoping for approval, which is depleting. The other is expecting other people to give us all we need as of right or a continuation of childhood; this completely stunts our growth, blocking the giving and receiving pipe. Neither of these mistakes feels pleasant for the person who is acting that way. When we give generously without expecting return, we naturally receive because the pipe is open and flowing. The trick is to find the enjoyment for yourself, and exploring the House and Sign of your Jupiter can give clues as to what activity will supply that enjoyment.

Exercise:

Search out an activity that relates to the style of Sign and House that contain Jupiter in your chart; make sure that you allow yourself the enjoyment of exploring that activity. Practise enjoying whatever you do. Look for the enjoyable part of every situation and focus on that, noticing what new ways you find to do things. Notice when fear stops you and, without being foolhardy, see if you can encourage yourself to follow through.

♄ Our sense of stability

Base centre, ***Saturn*** *(red) - consolidating energy for stability and perseverance*

Saturn represents our balance point, or tap root in the Earth, our foundation. Also it is the wisdom gained as we work to take responsibility for all our experiences in life. When we are children, adults have authority over us and discipline us, so we naturally project our Saturn onto them. We are projecting outside ourselves the energy of structuring and limiting, and we are predisposed to react to those situations and people in the way that the rest of the birth chart relates to Saturn. Some people never grow past that stage, and let us know by blaming other people for what they consider is wrong with life. The parent is reflected in the boss, or the government, or an irritating neighbour, anyone but themselves.

Blaming someone else for our troubles, we take the role of victim, powerless and out of control of our life. When we feel as adults that someone else has authority over us, we either become irresponsible children again or, in the small area where we may have power, we try to control through enforcing rigid, inflexible behaviour and rules.

Until we have endeavoured to establish some mastery of the Saturn Sign through self-discipline, we will feel a sense of insecurity which will limit our ability to be the authority in our own lives. We will fear difficult experience (victim mode), or feel anxiety about failure (the hard time we give ourselves). We gain the power of true authority only by accepting that everything in our life belongs to us, it all fits us in some way or it would not be there. One way or another, we created it, either by choosing on one level to experience it, or simply through the way we read life with our particular assumptions and expectations

As a guide, Saturn will not let us step out into the power of success unless we are secure in our own self. In practice this shows as the structures, circumstances and necessities of our life. So the Saturn Sign shows our style of inner work, of self-discovery or self-remembering. It shows how we persevere with the systematic uncovering of our unconsciousness, helping to clear the crown (Moon) chakra.

☽ ↓ ♄

As this inner work proceeds, the light of consciousness travels down the spine to waken the energy lying coiled and waiting at the base chakra. As it rises, that light creates the staff on which we can rely, a vibrant strength of our own, and the inner wisdom that guides us. That sense of inner strength enables us to be responsive to situations, maturity allows for flexibility. We know we will always be able to cope with life because we allow life to teach us how

♄ ♊

Saturn in Gemini is about learning to govern the processes of your mind. If you have Mercury in Pisces, say, this will not be an easy task because your natural method of thought is very unfocused and without logic. But whenever there is a self-disciplined effort to think clearly, the logic can be formidable - Saturn drawing the lines of reason inexorably. Saturn in Gemini goes more easily with Mercury in Aquarius, for example, showing a mind that normally thinks in organised patterns.

♄ ♏

A person with Saturn in Scorpio is being asked to look for their tap root in the deepest emotions. They will have been born knowing, or learned in childhood, that it wasn't safe to express that level of feeling. So the tendency is to keep it all under control, if that is possible. For a sense of inner security they will need to learn to be aware of what the emotions are, and what to do with them: they will be taking responsibility for them rather than blaming someone else. This will give them a stature with others that makes them believable in positions as counselors, psychotherapists, or overseeing people in any capacity.

♄♓ Saturn in Pisces, the Sign of no boundaries, indicates a childhood where discipline was unclear, finding boundaries a puzzle. In later life there is a tendency to express rules dogmatically and then change them. This is a person who will be strengthened by locating a familiar set of spiritual or humanitarian principles to live by. They may need to shut other people out of their space at times in order to persevere with the necessary work to achieve their goals.

♄□ Any personal planet square to Saturn will indicate a part of the personality that tends to be antagonised or hurt by authority, depending which planet and where it is placed. This also tends to show a difficulty with self-discipline, and yet systematic efforts to be organised will be rewarded with great achievements. As with all Square aspects, once the two work together, a new energy is released. For instance, Saturn in Aquarius Square Mercury in Scorpio, as an emotional way of looking at life that sees authority as cold and hard, when working together could produce a humanitarian speaker capable of moving the hardest heart.

Other aspects from Saturn tend to show a sense of anxiety and lack of confidence until the person has become proficient in their field somewhat later in life. This will go along with a softening of manner because it is the tension of fear that creates the rigid control. Saturn Conjunct, Sextile or Trine a personal planet is likely to reflect a person who seemed old and wise even in the cradle.

An unaspected Saturn shows a personality that can only get things organised on their own. It is very important for those people to know that, because if they try to work like others, they will develop a sense of being totally incapable of organising anything. Yet when no other part of the personality is being triggered by other people, they will actually be more efficient than most because there are no inner distractions.

So Saturn is about taking responsibility for what we experience in our lives, recognising that the way our life seems to be is a result of what we expect, and of how we are determined to see. As we accept this, taking care not to identify with what we have created or with the personality that creates it, we will find our true identity rooted in the Oneness of all life.

Exercise:

Look at your life in terms of the rules you felt you had to obey, the things you thought you had to do or must not do. The element Saturn is in will give a clue as to the level of life where you felt restricted. Then systematically work out what you gained through being limited in those ways. Accept the way it has been, and then ask yourself if some of those rules could be changed, and which rules you would prefer.

Outer planets in aspect to the inner seven

The outer planets are easier to understand in a birth chart if we look at them in relationship with the inner seven. It is as though the outer planets are teaching us their principles through specific chakra connections. If there is no aspect between an outer planet and any of the chakra planets in the birth chart, that outer planetary principle will not have a high priority in the person's consciousness. The principle will tend to arise as an issue only when that outer planet triggers a chakra planet through its movement, its transit, through the Zodiac. This might be experienced as a surprise inner change or event in life.

There follow some examples of outer planets aspecting chakra planets. When these aspects feel uncomfortable, it indicates that we are having trouble understanding the relevance of the planets' impersonal principles. What is needed is often a different way of looking at what appears to be going on.

♅

Uranus is teaching us about the principle of freedom.

In our bodies Uranus rules the nervous system. When it is in relationship with Mars in a birth chart, it is indicating that the energy this person uses is largely nervous energy. It feels exciting or frightening depending on one's attitude to change.

♅ + ♂

A Square aspect, Opposition or Quincunx to Mars, shows that the person's nervous system will tend to be depleted by the speedy way they go at life, so that they become very tense and subsequently exhausted. There is a need for this person to respect their nervous system as though it were a hothouse plant, give themselves the relevant food and vitamins, and regularly allow themselves times of freedom from inner pressure to relax with a massage, time off to read a book, or whatever works.

♅+♀

Uranus in aspect to Venus will be referring to feelings of separation in relationship which will usually have a sense of either loneliness or aloneness. A Trine or Sextile shows an easy sense of detachment which is a helpful quality in jobs like counselling, partly because we feel safer talking to someone who seems to be unaffected by what we are saying, and partly because the person with the aspect will not deplete themselves by worrying about clients in their free time.

A Square, Opposition or Quincunx shows that issues of abandonment and loss may be left over from traumatic experiences early this life and before, and there could be a fear of separating from a loved one. This person could be much supported knowing that on the mental/ emotional levels of life we are always together with those we love. If they have been clinging to relationship, with the unconscious fear that they cannot survive on their own, they may need freedom from it. Only in that space may they discover that they are great enough to cope with their own suffering personality, which may well dispense with most of the suffering.

♅+☿

In relationship with Mercury, Uranus indicates an electrical quality of mental activity. They will produce flashes of inspired vision alternating with blank patches. Uncomfortable aspects indicate difficulty dealing with the blanks, which may ease when the person learns to ask inwardly and wait for the answers to become clear. The silence of the blanks allows insights to arise.

Whether we feel the need for freedom or a fear of being freed, we need to be aware that both attitudes trap us into particular emotions and choices of behaviour. True inner freedom comes through a non-judgemental acceptance of what is there so that we are not pulled by those instinctive emotional reactions.

♆ **Neptune** is teaching us about the oneness of all life and the principle of trust that is needed to approach it.

An aspect from Neptune to Mercury, Venus or Mars, Sun or Moon, will indicate a person who has no boundaries between themselves and others. This means that they easily empathise, intuit others thoughts or emotions, and tend to pick up, without noticing, other people's issues.

△ The Trine indicates that the person is unaware of it as a problem and expects others to be equally sensitive. The □ Square indicates a person who finds it a problem, feeling themselves oversensitive, and invaded by others. Another difficulty stemming from a lack of boundaries is the person's tendency to trespass on the space of others, because they feel their space is everywhere .

To merge and become one with life, we need to completely relax, to trust life inwardly. When Neptune is Square to a more personal planet, it indicates a person who tends to misplace that trust by not paying attention to their intuition. They have very high ideals that they try to live up to, and hope that other people will live up to them too. Trying to live up to high ideals often means not accepting behaviour in ourselves or others that we consider to be less than ideal. When a person does this, they tend to attract people who mirror to them their own rejected qualities. In presenting a false impression, this person is deceived by others in return, or misreads them by giving them 'the benefit of the doubt'. When others act out those rejected qualities, the person feels disappointed, let down, even betrayed.

What is needed here is acceptance of the way we, and other people, actually are, even though we may not know what that is; this is our starting point. Ideals are like stars to a sailor, to guide our choices in the world. If we reject the way things are in favour of the way we would like them to be, we have no starting point and we get lost.

Accepting ourselves the way we are means being totally honest with ourselves and with our world. When we do that, people can't help revealing themselves to us, we get to see who they are, and we are not later surprised by them.

When people speak of trusting someone, it often means that they expect a certain behaviour of them, which is unfair. We need to trust ourselves in relationship with life, trust that we will be able to handle whatever situations arise, no matter whether people fulfil our expectations of them or not. It is the essential self in each person that we can trust as being part of the essence of life.

♆ □ ♂

Neptune Square Mars shows a person who is extremely sensitive to others to their own detriment. As Mars corresponds to the solar plexus, we may suffer from stomach tension as an effort to prevent ourselves always reacting to others' emotions. This reservoir of energy can be misdirected because we think we know what others are feeling and why; and with Neptune Square, although we pick up correct information, there is a tendency to misinterpret it according to our fears.

We need to be more aware of our own feelings while with others, to steady ourselves, and when feeling guilty about another person's hurt or anger, to remember that we may well not be the cause. Because personalities, by their nature, are separate, any sense of blending with another personality is an illusion. We may be projecting our identity onto them because they mirror us so well; or we may be overlapping their space so that we feel their feelings and think their thoughts, and we must be careful not to lose ourselves in their issues, or clutter their space with our feelings and thoughts.

As the veils between our understanding and the reality of Oneness gradually disappear, we may experience confusion and increased sensitivity in the element and

House Neptune occupies in our chart, and through the placing of the chakra planet aspected by Neptune. We may experience psychic phenomena, informative dreams, or increased spiritual awareness depending on our level of operation. True blending can only be with that which is common to all existence, spirit, or the essence of life itself.

♇ **Pluto** is teaching us about the attitude required to allow the transformation of our identity from our separate personality towards universal spirit, as the caterpillar transforms into a butterfly, its identiy as caterpillar dying in the process.

Being about death and transformation, Pluto tends to be feared. There is in most of us the desire to control the way things are in order to avoid that death, because, from the personality point of view, the transformation is not understood. Each person's particular terrors are shown by Pluto's position in the birth chart, and the planets that it aspects will be the chakras that we try to control. We fear that this death will come from outside, so maintaining control feels essential to survival, but we are actually projecting our power into our world instead of recognising it as ours, which is why the world seems so frightening.

We use manipulation, domination, and all kinds of power games to hold the death away. Like a lid on the volcano, this is no use, and the longer we hold it down, the bigger the explosion in the end. Pluto's aim is to penetrate us to the roots, bringing into the open all that we have tried to hide away, because with transformation nothing is left untouched. Usually the transformation comes about through a situation that develops or arrives in life that we cannot deal with at our old level. There is a need for us to accept that, like a growing snake, we too will feel more comfortable, more ourselves, when we allow our outgrown skin, attitudes, assumptions, judgements, to fall away. Pluto Trine a planet shows that there is an acceptance of the ♇△ principle. The transformations are still not easy, but they tend to be understood as they are happening. Pluto Squares □ show a harder fight, clinging to the past more desperately. The identity is so fixed in some aspect of the personality that it feels as though we ourselves will not survive if we let it go.

Pluto aspects to Venus are about clinging to ♇+♀ relationship obsessively until the other person feels suffocated and leaves, or rejecting relationships so that we do not have to suffer being rejected; any expectations of disaster cause the Venus to create disaster. There is a need here for the feminine aspect of the personality to be given tender loving care by oneself, to be appreciated and healed in spite of the negative emotions that it contains. Sometimes this is easier to do by seeing Venus in the Sign she occupies, visualising her as a separate character in a life where the triggering trauma took place. Once she is acknowledged she can tell of her pain, and we can accept and love her.

Any outer experience of rejection is simply a reflection of what we are doing already to ourselves: if we accept ourselves, however unacceptable we fear we may be, we will see that other people are not rejecting us in truth; they, like us, are dealing with their own problems in the only ways they know how. Having found and accepted the fearing, possessive, suffering part of ourselves, we can see beyond it, which may quite largely be the transformation itself.

Pluto requires that we be prepared to let go of past memories and all future plans. We need to develop an attitude of completely open adaptability to the power of the moment, and whatever events and changes it brings. We need to let go our attachment to every characteristic of the person we have thought ourselves to be. Transforming, we will be different, and there is no way of knowing beforehand how we will be afterwards.

⚷

Chiron is teaching us that we are not separate from each other, and that the moment we reach beyond our pain to give to another, we start to heal our wounds.

Whichever planets Chiron aspects in the chart tend to be facets of character that seem to be damaged at birth. Squares, Oppositions and Quincunxes are likely to be more damaged, but Trines and Sextiles will also be painfully affected. The wounded feeling can range from a slight lack of confidence around those characteristics, to a fear of expressing them at all which freezes our energy. Because Chiron is a fairly recent discovery, I am giving here notes on all the possible Zodiac positions, developed by exploring people's experience while reading their charts. My promptings to make this enquiry are, not surprisingly, reflected by Chiron having prime placing in my own birth chart!

For each of the twelve Zodiac placings of Chiron, these are four questions one could ask about the person. The answers to the first of these questions show the wonderful work that people can achieve even though they began this life feeling small and helpless, hiding from the pains that seemed to be always inflicted by an insensitive world. Those gifts arise as each individual recognises a common humanity with others and, with compassion, speaks out what they know in spite of possible ridicule or reprisals, or does what is needed in the face of apparently frowning tradition.

Through their courage, they bring healing to people and situations, and as they move forward in this way they are in fact supported by life. It is this that brings the longed-for healing: an end to the negativity they pour over themselves.

In any individual case, the answers will be more complex than those given here, due to other planetary aspects and the specific Houses involved. It should also be remembered, as always, that a person's experience is unique to them, and an astrologer can only point to the kind of feeling they might have.

Four questions for Chiron in a birth chart:

1 What is their gift to humanity, their method of healing?

2 What do they fear from the outside that seems to do the damage?

3 If the gift is damaged so that they lack confidence, what do they feel as a result?

4 How do they protect themselves from more hurt - their survival mode, self-protection?

Chiron in each Sign would have different answers to these four questions. On the next pages are some suggested answers. Do check these thoughts against your own experience and that of other people. Chiron is a relatively recent addition to birth chart readings and its meaning is still being discovered. Your findings are as valid as those of anyone else.

⚷ ♈ Chiron in Aries

Their gift	1	Encouraging independence
their fear	2	Others' lack of faith in them
their pain	3	Nervousness
protection	4	Being competitive

⚷ ♉ Chiron in Taurus

Their gift	1	Steady, physical healing
their fear	2	Loss of things
their pain	3	Insecurity
protection	4	Possessiveness

⚷ ♊ Chiron in Gemini

Their gift	1	Speaking their truth
their fear	2	Being misunderstood
their pain	3	That they can't communicate
protection	4	Talking too much

⚷ ♋ Chiron in Cancer

Their gift	1	Emotionally nurturing
their fear	2	Being neglected
their pain	3	That nobody cares
protection	4	Huffy

⚷ ♌ Chiron in Leo

Their gift	1	Positive, inspiring
their fear	2	Ridicule
their pain	3	The inner fire out
protection	4	Hiding or controlling

⚷ ♍ Chiron in Virgo

Their gift	1	Painstaking caring for people
their fear	2	Criticism of mistakes
their pain	3	Uselessness
protection	4	Over-analytical

Chiron in Libra

Their gift	1	Diplomatic with integrity
their fear	2	Rejection
their pain	3	Lonely
protection	4	Try too hard to please

Chiron in Scorpio

Their gift	1	Deeply understanding
their fear	2	Emotional attack
their pain	3	Constantly in emotional pain
protection	4	Hide feelings

Chiron in Sagittarius

Their gift	1	Freeing minds from orthodoxy
their fear	2	Criticism of ideas
their pain	3	Fear of freedom
protection	4	Argumentative

Chiron in Capricorn

Their gift	1	Fearless handling of changes
their fear	2	Others' lack of faith in their ability
their pain	3	Incompetent, victim
protection	4	Will not get involved

Chiron in Aquarius

Their gift	1	Faith in human value
their fear	2	Being let down or forcibly cut off
their pain	3	Disillusioned
protection	4	Cynicism

Chiron in Pisces

Their gift	1	Empathic service through merging
their fear	2	Being swamped or hurt
their pain	3	Worthlessness
protection	4	Shy

We are not separate from spirit

Every planet represents a spiritual quality. Qualified through its placing in a Zodiac Sign and House, its energy reflects part of the personality. When we harbour a mistaken belief of thinking ourselves separate from our source, we clutter ourselves with feelings of guilt and fear, the need for attack and defence, and a host of consequent negatives.

In feeling separate, we judge our energy to be wrong, shameful, unacceptable, denying our spirit's acceptance of all that we are. The result is a sense of personality that is divided, with some planets reflecting beautiful virtues and others 'dreadful defects'. We set them against each other to do battle within ourselves seeing their relationships, or aspects, as either good or bad.

What we can do to release ourselves from the battle, both externally and internally, is to accept our world and our personality as they are, and as reflected by the birth chart, always remembering that we *have* a personality, it is not who we *are*. The consequent relief brings relaxation which allows the love of life to flow through us, naturally refining the planetary qualities into a bridge to our essential self.

That Self is spirit unbounded, at one with all existence.

Chapter 4
The Houses

Part 1
Ways in which we are the same

It is perfectly possible to read a birth chart without knowing the *time* of birth. When we have only the *date* of birth, the astrological information available will be the positions of the planets in their Signs, to within a degree or so of accuracy, and their relationships, or aspects, to each other. However, the Moon moves from 12 to 15 degrees (half a Sign) during the 24 hours of the birth day, so its position cannot be so accurate.

From this information, an astrologer will be able to interpret the style of the person's energy, what they can express well or with difficulty, what their life and relationships feel like on the inside, and the timing of major life shifts to within a year. What will be unknown is the particular areas of life where all this energy expresses itself, whether it is in work or with friends or at home. Also unknown are the month by month timings possible from the precise placing of the Moon.

Knowing the time of birth, we can calculate what was rising over the horizon, the Ascendent, and the

Midheaven, giving us the twelve Houses which enable us to place each planetary energy in a specific area of life.

Not many people know the exact time of their birth to the minute; many times are given on the hour or half-hour, which seems a little approximate. But my experience is that when a time is given, the chart for that time seems to give the information that is helpful to the person at the time of the reading. If a person feels uncertain of the birth time they are giving, one can construct a chart for the approximate time, and still give a useful interpretation.

A bit of astronomy - the physical Houses

The Earth is perpetually rolling over towards the Eastern sky. Each one of us sits on this beautiful ball watching the sky roll overhead, rising in the East. The planets move slowly through their orbits round the Sun, while the Sun occupies a stationary place in the centre of its system of planets. The Earth rolls along its orbit round the Sun, turning completely over in about 23 hours 56 minutes.

Sitting on the Earth, if we were to watch the stars by night and measure our time by, say, Sirius, we would find that Sirius would be due South approximately every 23 hours 56 minutes; however, we actually measure our time by watching the Sun. As we have moved each day about one degree further through our orbit round the Sun, the Sun itself appears to us about one degree further through the Zodiac than the previous day. Thus the Sun appears to have travelled 361 degrees. That extra degree takes the 4 minutes needed to complete the 24 hours of our day in Earth Time. Similarly, the 360 degrees of the Zodiac is also divided into 24 hours, but we call that Sidereal Time as opposed to Earth Time.

Depending when your spirit 'decides' it is right to come out of your earthly mother, the Earth will be at a particular point in her rolling, and a particular part of the sky will be rising over the horizon. If it is night where your mother is, the Sun will be below the Earth, so if a chart is drawn for that moment with the horizon across the middle of the circle, the Sun will be drawn below the line.

To draw the chart we are looking South, so the rising degree is on the left. The First House begins at that rising point and refers to that area of sky rising next, so it is below the horizon. The Second and subsequent Houses follow it, and so are numbered anticlockwise.

The Midheaven or Medium Coeli (MC) is above the horizon. It refers to the degree of the Zodiac belt on the local meridian, that imaginary line from North to South at the chart location. In most systems of House division, the MC begins the 10th House, so all twelve Houses derive from the horizon and the local meridian. These two lines cut the chart into four sections, each containing three Houses.

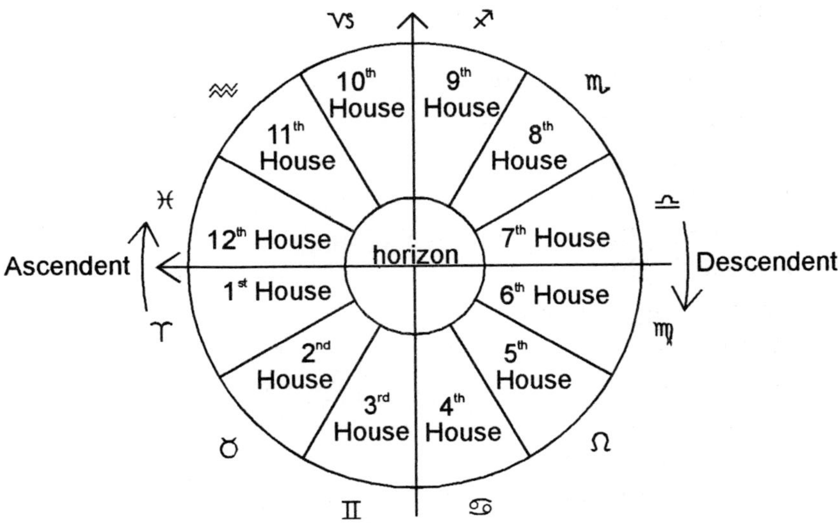

The horizon indicates our relationship with what we find around us. The beginning (the cusp) of the First House is called the Ascendent and indicates how we are predisposed to see the world around us, and also our appearance, our behaviour or interface with what we see. The Descendent (cusp of the 7th House) indicates what qualities of relationship our behaviour attracts in order to balance our Ascendent qualities. The MC (cusp of the 10th House) shows what we see as ideal, and therefore reach to achieve for ourselves. The Immum Coeli or IC (cusp of the 4th House) is the foundation that we stand on to reach those ideals, our early life and sense of security.

The twelve Houses through which we experience the world

The twelve Houses divide the full circle of our world, describing what we are looking towards, the different areas of our life experience, as follows:
(In brackets are the particular relationships that tend to be associated with those areas.)

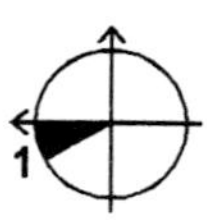

First House -
new situations, my appearance, the way others see me
(people - those I am just meeting)

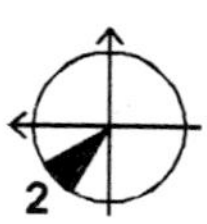

Second House -
my possessions, my personal money and income, my immediate environment, the house I live in, my body, the things I value
(people - those I live with, those who occupy the same house)

Third House -
communication with that which is near to me, through speech, writing or movement, local journeys

(people - my relatives, siblings, school friends, neighbours)

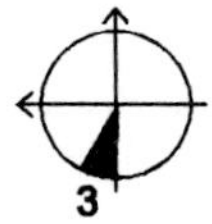

Fourth House -
home, where I feel at home, my nest, my roots, land

(people - the family into which I was born, least known parent - tends to be father)

Fifth House -
creative outlets and ventures, hobbies, recreation, entertainment, pleasure, romance

(people - children, lovers, all creative works)

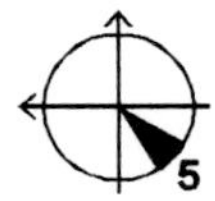

Sixth House -
routines of daily life, job, work, health, service to others

(people - colleagues, employees, pets, clients, those I serve or who serve me)

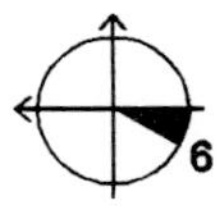

Seventh House -
my relationship with my world

(people - my close friends, my partner, my spouse, 'other half', the other person in any one-to-one relationship)

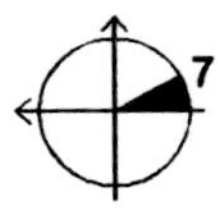

Eighth House -
other people's money, inheritance, shared resources, the underlying rules of relationship, business partnership, ecology of the Earth, opportunities to transform myself through relationship

(people - business partners, deeply emotionally close partners, those who challenge my control)

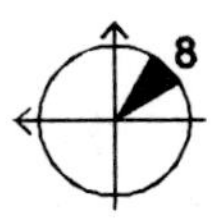

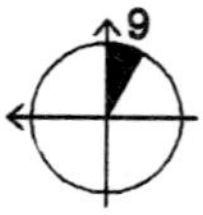

Ninth House -
chosen field of study, higher education, philosophy, religion, the principles I was brought up on, law, long journeys, travel

(people - teachers, those whose ideas influenced me philosophically, religious inspirer, guru, my in-laws)

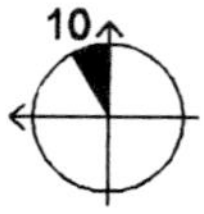

Tenth House -
vocation, career, public face, reputation, fame

(people - the most known parent who tends to be mother, those with qualities I admire, boss)

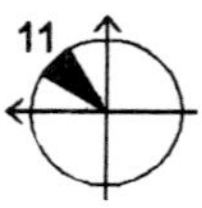

Eleventh House -
society, the world 'out there', groups, clubs, the audience, the public

(people - open friendships, acquaintances, group spirit)

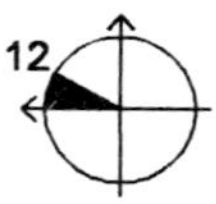

Twelfth House -
the unknown, dreams, institutions, events and personality that come forward into this life directly from past lives

(people - unseen companions, guides, those who are absent or hidden, access to the unconscious)

Exercise:

Think of the many concerns, activities, people, in your life, and try to imagine which House would contain each one, through which window you would look to see them.

Creating our experience

Every aspect of our personal life, as we live it day by day, is like a window onto a greater life, life as it really is; but, if we need to look through windows, it is necessary that they be clean. We tend to take for granted that what the eye sees is a true representation of what is there, but the windows have been silting up for many lifetimes. All the negative thoughts people have in relation to an area of life leave their dust and grime on the window until eventually many people find that life is a bit boring and grey; the light of reality can hardly penetrate.

There is a need to clear away some of the results of past personal experience from our vision and, as we realise this, we begin a cleaning process. This may involve counselling or writing a journal day by day so that the little forgotten thoughts get more notice; it is often the *whispering background* to our thinking that gives away our true motives and emotional reactions stemming from childhood experiences and before. We may go to workshops on self-development, beginning to peel the onion of the personality to find the gold light in the centre. But often the *process* of cleaning takes over our attention. We focus on ourselves and our difficulties, almost forgetting the original desire to see through the windows and let the light in.

What is needed at that point is that we accept what we have discovered about ourselves, instead of trying to get rid of it. We realise that it is only our negative thinking and expectation of failure that make the windows *seem* dirty. When we change our attitude from negative to positive, playful, or adventuring, the dust and grime disappear. Our focus naturally shifts from continual thoughts of self to what is actually happening through the window.

The Houses in astrology represent those windows. They show the expectations that we have of how the world will be in those areas, what we expect to see. They also show our attitudes to those things, how we feel and what we think about them. A lot may be happening in a particular area of our life, but we tend to experience only that part that we recognise from our expectations. That is to say, we are defining, and even limiting, our experience with our own thinking.

Having realised this, there are two ways we can grow. One way is cleaning the windows: improving our experiences by being ourselves more positively so that life is more enjoyable. The other way is changing the focus so that the state of the window doesn't prevent us seeing what is really there: then we accept ourselves in the way spirit accepts, which dissolves the negativity, and possibly the window too. We can do either or both.

Improving experience starts with learning how we are creating the problems. We need to accept what it is that we are doing with our energy, how we are projecting ourselves out there, and we also need to practise doing things differently using the energy at our disposal; this is learning to use the tool kit of personality more skilfully. It can be done by discovering which of the planetary energies has been judged unacceptable or unattainable, and therefore projected out onto others. We need to see the virtue of each energy and how it can be safely used, and also to realise that we already have the qualities we admire in others. Then we can accept these parts of the personality more easily.

Changing the focus deliberately from the window of perception to what is beyond it requires a shift in personal identity, a spiritual awakening. Because we are spirit in truth, it is always possible in theory to identify with it, but even when we realise this as an idea, it is still necessary to develop the *aware experience* of ourselves as spirit. Realising it is the first great step, but we start from the awareness of ourselves as individuals, and identifying with spirit completely is to enter the Oneness within which there are no separate entities.

The movement towards the experience of oneness will be different for different people. For some it may be in stages from an vague awareness of inner guidance, to a conscious connection with Higher Self as a guide, later identifying with that Higher Consciousness. For others the process may be an undefined maturing, and for others, different again.

Throughout the process we develop qualities of feeling which are associated with spiritual awakening: compassion for those who used to irritate, joy for no apparent reason, a peaceful patience where we would have been tense, and so on. While those feelings are present we are in touch with that source of all life that is within. However, we may want to work at improving our use of personality at the same time.

Our birth chart helps us to know the structure of our chosen personality, which is a good beginning; but the principles of the planets and the Zodiac Signs are also pointers to spiritual qualities that we can achieve, so they can be used as keys to focusing beyond the glass. By developing the qualities of planets and Signs that are relevant to each House in our chart, we can open those windows on the world and get to see what is really there.

Exercise:

Practise wondering who people really are, especially when you think you know them.

The Houses

Part 2
Ways in which we are different

To open our windows on the world and get to see what is really there, we need to develop the qualities of planets and Signs that are relevant to each House in our individual chart. The way we use the Houses to describe our individuality is to look through each House window to see which part of the Zodiac was there at our time of birth.

The Sign at the beginning of each House gives the most effective description, followed by the chart position of its ruling planet. Any planet within that House will show a part of your energy that is triggered by the concerns of that House.

The Ascendent

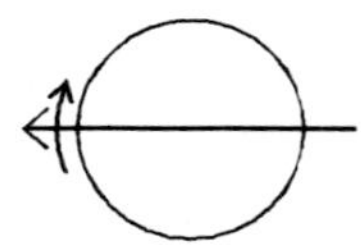

Any one of 360 degrees in the circle of 12 Zodiac Signs, could be rising at any moment for each place on the Earth. One of the Signs was rising at the moment you were born and the degree of that Sign exactly on the horizon is called your Ascendent. It will reflect your spirit's chosen way of relating to the world you see around you this life.

That rising Sign is your way of expressing yourself, your approach to new situations; it is that style with which you naturally greet each new person. If, for some reason, it is difficult for you to express that Sign, you will not come across very easily at all. It would be like losing the interface of your personality-computer with the user you are trying to meet. That person would look at you wondering what is going on, and may well lose interest. One way to deal with such a situation is to wait for the first moment to pass and then go straight into using one of the planetary energies, such as Mercury (speech) or Venus (warm receptivity) instead of assuming your Ascendent style is the only way.

If a planet was rising or about to rise at your birth, it will be shown on the Ascendent or in the First House in your birth chart, and will represent the nature of the energy that comes across from you in those new situations. If that planet is Mars, it indicates an energetic approach in the style of the Sign. So if Mars was in Scorpio, it would show that you come across with an emotional intensity in your energy which some people may step back from, unsure whether you are safe to approach. Others who have some of that style in their own nature, and are comfortable with it, are likely to feel attracted to you.

The Descendent and relationships

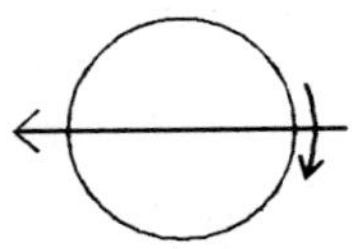

The Sign on the Ascendent represents the quality of our first approach to life. Interestingly, we tend to desire its complement in our relationships; we are attracted to people who have some qualities of the opposite Sign, that is the Descendent. It is as though we unconsciously feel the need for balance and, although we are ourselves obliquely expressing those Descending qualities, we are often not aware of it, and so we develop them in our close relationships.

For instance, a person with Libra rising will come across pleasantly, always prepared to follow the general consensus, willing to sacrifice their personal desires for the sake of peace. They will be attracted to people who know their own minds and who are likely to be forceful in ♈↓ expressing what they want, reflecting their own Aries on the Descendent. However, once they are in close relationship with someone expressing Aries, they become more like that themselves; and the person who was originally attracted to them, because of their Libran expression of gentleness and apparent flexibility, is suddenly surprised to find that they are not so easy going after all and want to do things their own way.

♉↑ Again, Taurus rising looks like someone who is ultimately steady, can be leaned on any time and will always support others with a strong shoulder. They have Scorpio descending, attracted to those with turbulent emotions who need steady support. However, once in close relationship, these people will begin to express the emotions that were ♏↓ held back when the steady qualities were being expressed; and then the relationship can be stormy, with extremes of up and down.

These descending qualities are a necessary expression for us in our relationships. The difficulty comes when we don't realise that we need to express those qualities ourselves. The Taurus rising person may think that ♌↑ they want stability and blame the partner for the storms. Leo rising may think they want fun and warmth all the time, and blame the Aquarian-style partner for being cold and ♒↓ distant, when in fact what Leo-rising needs is space and freedom in relationship to express their radiance in their own special way.

Once we realise that we need to express the Descending quality in our relationships, we are able to happily find relationships where the *positive* qualities of the descending Sign are expressed by both ourself and our partner. That Aquarian Descendent of a Leo-rising person will express as a natural giving of space, and time happily spent apart. The Scorpio Descendent of Taurus-rising will be a relationship in which deep emotions can be aired without shaking the foundations. The Aries Descendent of a Libra-rising person will indicate a couple who discuss equally what they will do, with give and take on both sides.

The planet which often confuses this understanding of what we need in a relationship is Venus, the energy of attraction. Venus reflects the energy we feel comfortable with when actively relating to people, and the style of affection we like to receive.

However, what we want is not always what we need, and it is much more worth while in terms of general happiness to uncover what we need and develop that. The Venus qualities will continue anyway as part of the chemistry of our relationships. Our need for a complement expressed by the Descendent is a large background issue.

For example, one who has Leo rising, and therefore Aquarius setting, and also Venus in Pisces, will have a need in relationship for the space expressed by the opposite Sign of Aquarius, even though the Venus may reflect a romantic desire for merging with the partner. In this case it is the space that is most important in order for a relationship to survive. Constant merging would stifle both partners, but occasional romantic interludes could add the excitement that an Aquarius relationship thrives on.

Our relationship with our world

We are each predisposed to see things in a certain way that is individual to our specific past experience, and our faculties of perception and interpretation. From a personality point of view, it is our expectations of what we will see through the windows that determines what we actually see. It follows that, when we look at our experiences in the world, what we are seeing is a reflection of our personality. So we will now examine the Houses in these two ways: firstly, how our attitudes and expectations create our experience; and secondly, how our experience reflects our personality.

It is the Zodiac Sign at the beginning (on the cusp) of each House that shows our attitude to that part of our world. The Sign on the cusp is the primary indicator of how we feel about that area of life, what kind of experiences we expect when engaged in those activities, and therefore what we actually experience happening to us. Our life will be this way because this is the way we expect it to be.

Wonderfully, once we know this, we can begin to let go of our expectations and become prepared to be surprised.

The Houses: How our attitudes and expectations create our experience

The Sign on the cusp of a House (at the beginning of the House) in our own chart and the chart position of the planet ruling that Sign show our attitude to the concerns of that House. They show how we expect experience to be in that area of life (active energy), and what we see coming back to us (passive perception). In each case our perceived experience will confirm our suspicions.

In the following section, an example is given for each House with a particular Sign on the cusp (e.g. 1st House - Scorpio). In practice, the cusp of the first House could be in any Sign.

1st House -

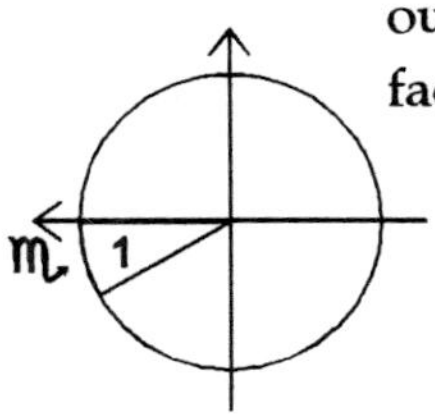

our attitude to ourself, how we expect to be when facing life; what life looks like to us

(e.g. Scorpio: I am vulnerable when I approach life - life hurts, in the area where Pluto is.)

2nd House -

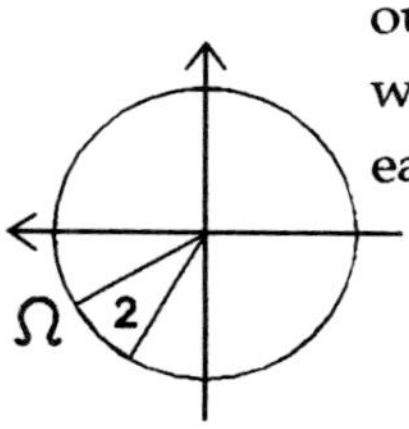

our attitude to the physical world in general, what we feel we deserve; what we receive by way of earnings, what we value about ourselves

(e.g. Leo: I enjoy my possessions - my income describes my worth through the Sun's House activity, I value my self-expression in the Sun's House.)

3rd House -

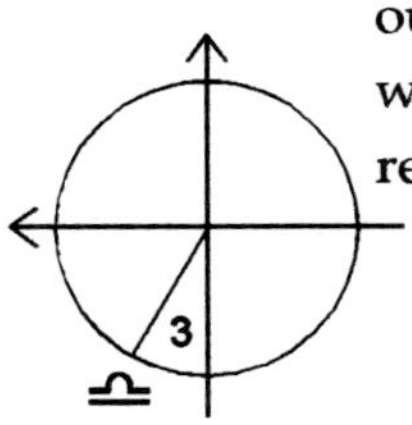

our attitude to learning and communication, how we expect people to talk; how we see people reacting to us

(e.g. Libra: speech should be diplomatic - people like relating to me about the concerns of the Venus House.)

4th House -

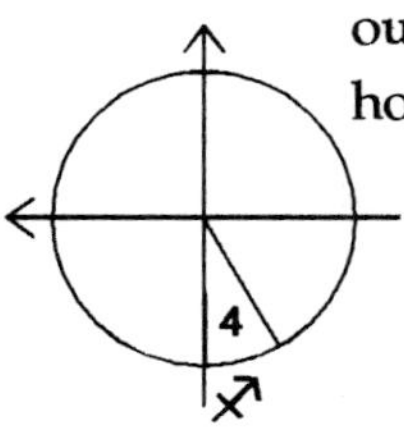

our attitude to our early life, how we expect our home to be; how father seemed to be

(e.g. Sagittarius: my home is interesting - father was fun, in Jupiter House ways.)

5th House -

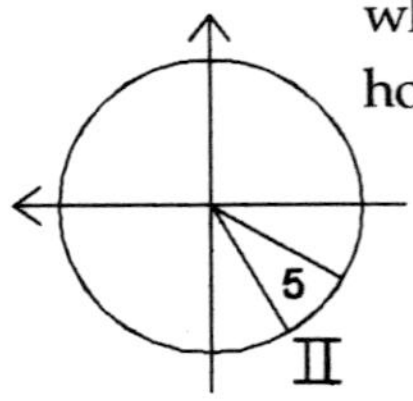

our attitude to creativity in ourselves and others, what we expect from love affairs and from children; how affairs pan out, how children behave with us

(e.g. Gemini: fun with words, storytelling; variety triggers creativity; I talk to children as equals - children chat to me about things of Mercury's House.)

6th House -

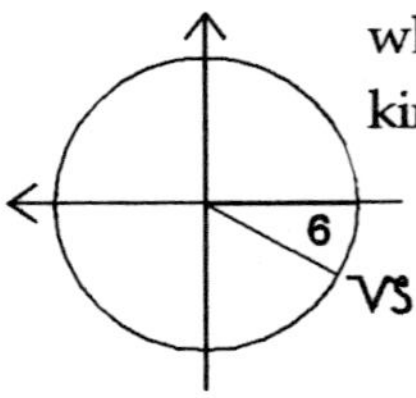

our attitude to the routines of life, to our health, what we expect our working conditions to be; the kind of jobs we get, what affects our health

(e.g. Capricorn: it is important to be organised - I get responsible jobs, in the field of Saturn's House.)

7th House -

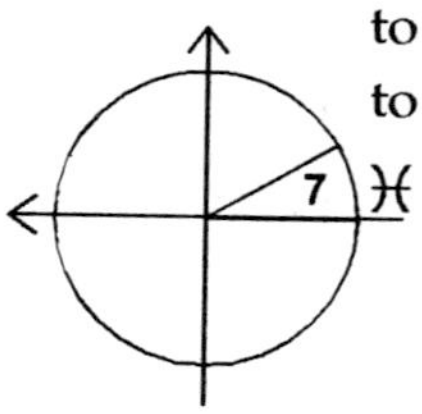

our attitude to our partner or spouse, how we expect them to behave; the issues we seem to have to deal with in relationship, how our partner seems to be

(e.g. Pisces: my partner should know how I feel- we are so intuitive, especially about Neptune House concerns.)

8th House -

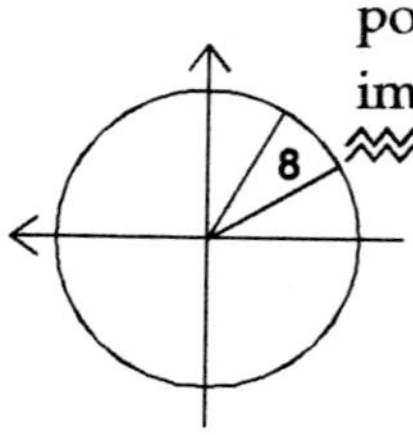

our attitude to other people's values and possessions, what we expect to get from any important partnership; power struggles

(e.g. Aquarius: equality of ownership - clear rules, about freedom in the issues of Uranus' House.)

9th House -

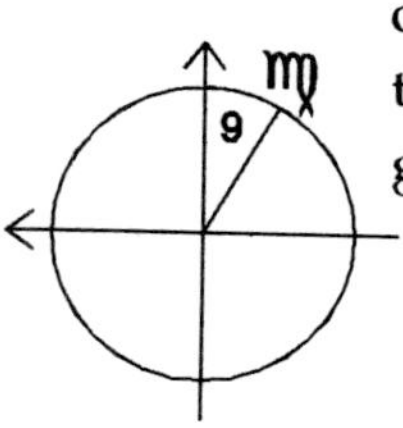

our attitude to life, to religion, to study and teaching, how we expect teachers to be; the way we gather knowledge and understanding of life

(e.g. Virgo: people should help each other - I study hard, in the House of Mercury.)

10th House -

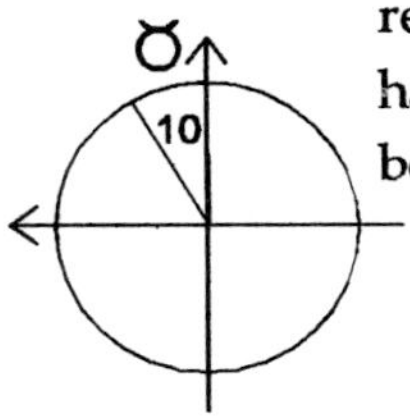

our attitude to our career, to our top priorities, the results we expect when going for our ideals; what happens when we do our best, how mother seems to be

(e.g. Taurus: a career should be safe - I succeed if I relate, in the Venus House.)

11th House -

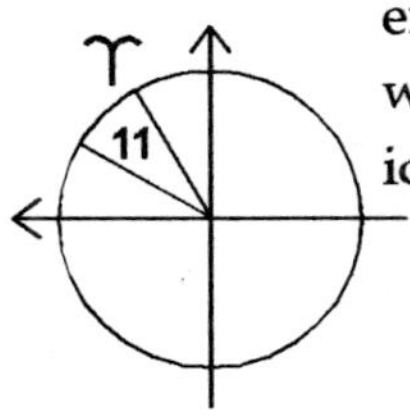

our attitude to groups of people, to society, how we expect to be treated in group situations; the way the world seems to treat us, what happens when we identify with a group

(e.g. Aries: each person in a group should be responsible for themselves - my contribution will be what I want to do, in the Mars House.)

12th House -

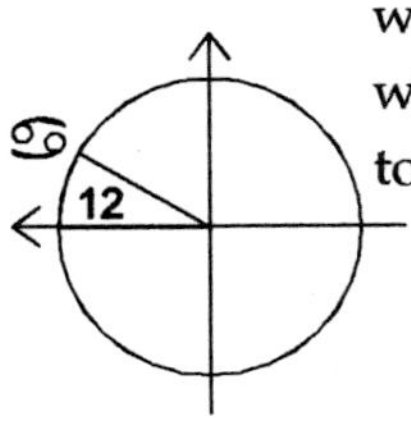

our attitude to the unknown, to being alone, what we expect to be missing in the world around us; what we seem to be without in childhood and have to find within ourselves.

(e.g. Cancer: being on our own is nurturing - I meditate when I am involved in the activities of the House containing the Moon.)

Exercise:

Practise imagining the attitude of other Signs at the beginning (the cusp) of each House.

"By accepting myself as I am, and the world and people around me as my reflection, my struggle with life fades. As I relax, I enjoy my life more and the reflection gently becomes nearer what I would like it to be; my experience changes."

The Houses: How our experience reflects our personality

The Sign on the cusp and the chart position of the planet ruling that Sign show how I feel I am, and need to be, in order to meet the challenges of that House well. If I can accept that my personality equipment is like this, and allow myself to express these qualities, a great deal of the struggle and difficulty goes out of my life immediately, and other people will accept me as I feel myself to be. If I allow my personality to be the way it prefers, I relax and others relax around me, more easily able to be themselves too.

In the next section, the examples of Signs on the House cusp are the same as used previously.

1st House -

who I think I am, my way of approaching the world, reflected in what the world seems to be about

(I need to approach life this way. e.g. Scorpio on the cusp: sensitive at a deep level)

2nd House -
how I feel about myself, my sense of worth, what I value in myself, reflected in what the world pays me for what I do

(I need to feel that these qualities are valuable. e.g. Leo on the cusp: positivity and fun)

3rd House -
how I communicate, my way of interacting, reflected in the way people react when I speak

(I need to communicate things in this way. e.g. Libra on the cusp: gently, pleasantly)

4th House -
my private face, childhood impressions, fundamental emotional security, reflected in my home life

(I need this to feel secure. e.g. Sagittarius on the cusp: reasons why)

5th House -
my sense of enjoyment, my self expression as creative, how I play, reflected in my creations

(I need this to feel happy. e.g. Gemini on the cusp: communication)

6th House -
my feelings about organising my daily life, how I 'get it together', reflected in my health, and in my work situation

(I need this in order to be organised. e.g. Capricorn on the cusp: a sensible work situation)

7th House -
what I feel I don't have so need another person to supply, reflected in the behaviour of my partner to me

(I need to be this way in close relationships. e.g. Pisces on the cusp: letting my feelings flow)

8th House -

my depths, my efforts to transform in relation to others, my desire for control, for autonomy in deep relationships, reflected in people's reactions to me when I reveal my depths

> (I need to treat my deepest issues this way. e.g. Aquarius on the cusp: with detachment)

9th House -

my sense of meaning and purpose, my search for a map or guidelines, reflected in my teachers

> (I need these kind of guidelines. e.g. Virgo on the cusp: precise)

10th House -

my highest priorities, what I desire the world to acknowledge in me, to achieve, reflected in those I admire

> (I need to feel appreciated for this. e.g. Taurus on the cusp: my stability)

11th House -

how I feel about the world, how I see myself in relation to everyone out there, reflected in the groups I join

> (I need to express these qualities in groups. e.g. Aries on the cusp: independence, directness)

12th House -

my inner world, my atmosphere, what I search for outside and fail to find, what I am blended with so much that I have difficulty identifying it, reflected in my meditation experiences, in my dreams

> (I need to connect with this kind of inner guidance. e.g. Cancer on the cusp: kind and loving)

Exercise:

These examples used the same Signs as the previous list. Complete this list imagining the attitude of the Signs you used before, and notice the different feeling for the person who may have this Sign on the cusp.

So, my personality moulds the way I see life. My mistake is to think that life really is the way I perceive it. Sometimes, in the midst of my reactions to what I perceive as happening to me, I can have a quiet inner sense that things are not what they seem. In that inner part of myself I am recognising that the people I am reacting to are actually just being themselves, and they may not mean what I think they mean. At this point I can begin to have a living relationship with the world as it is, and not just with my thoughts and feelings about it.

Planets in the Houses

Any planet in a House shows the energy we put directly into those concerns, and also the way we experience them. For instance:

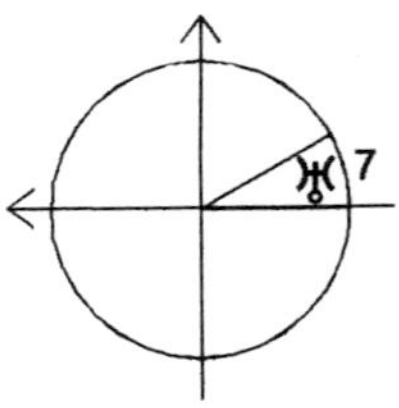

a) Uranus in the 7th House may say, "I want to be free in relationships" and the experience tends to be of relating to someone who is not there much of the time, or of many changes in relationship.

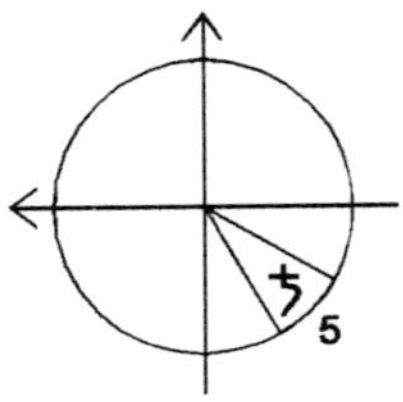

b) An uncomfortably aspected Saturn in the 5th House may say, "I'm not old enough, or stable enough, to handle the responsibility of having children" and they would be very likely to leave the disciplining to their spouse; when they have to take charge, they would tend to compensate for the sense of weakness by being overly heavy or controlling.

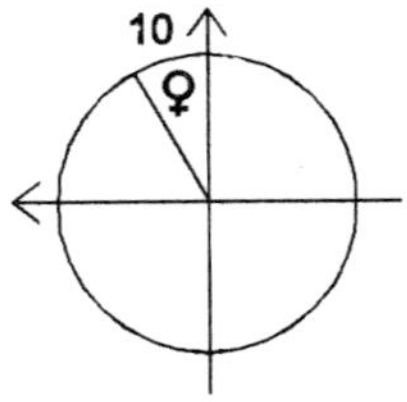

c) Venus in the 10th House may say, "I want everybody to love me" and they present attractiveness to the world, pleasant manners, social aptitude, and the world loves them.

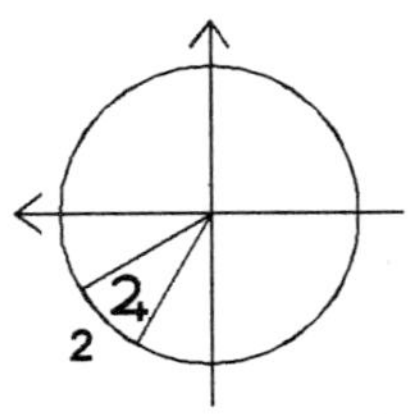

d) Jupiter in the 2nd House says, "Money? easy come, easy go!" and they experience little problem in earning enough for their needs, maybe much more, and spending or giving away all they get.

There follows a little about each planet in relation to its effect on the House it occupies in a birth chart.

Sun: ☉

The House that contains the Sun in a chart is of prime importance. Bearing in mind that the Sun represents our central self, and allows the spirit entry into everyday life, it is necessary not only to be one's Sun Sign but also to be active in the House.

Sun in Capricorn in the 3rd House, shows a person who needs not only to express competence and serious carefulness, but also to express it in words to people.

Sun in Aquarius in the 2nd House, may show a person who has the welfare of all members of society at heart, and also needs to be paid for working in that field, if they are to value themselves.

This latter is the kind of situation where a person can negate their sense of worthiness as an individual, because their principles seem to deny what they personally need. It is here that knowing their birth chart can be such a relief, because it will validate their own needs so that they are able to see the principle in perspective.

The person relevant to the House containing the Sun (see the list in Part 1 of this Chapter), is the one to whom we tend to give our light away, so that they become the source of light and life, we fall in love, give our heart away:
Sun in the 5th House does this to the lover or the child;
Sun in the 6th, to the client;
Sun in the 2nd, to the acquisition of possessions;
Sun in the 9th, to the teacher or religious leader.

When we do this, that person's opinion can make or break us, we feel we cannot live without them, and we need to draw back that power. Being and appreciating ourselves in the area of life of the Sun's House helps us to achieve that return of the light to our own heart centre where it has to be.

☽ Moon:

Whichever House contains the Moon is that area of life that instinctively occupies us.

Moon in the 8th House shows a person who will always be reacting to the deepest level of life situations. That reaction may be light chat about the situation if Moon is in Gemini, or seeing the positive or funny side if in Leo. Their mother may have had that perspective herself, which would have been part of the attraction for this particular spirit to be the child, so that the characteristic would be embedded in the upbringing. This 8th House Moon will tend to take it for granted that those around them are involved in deep issues; how the Moon is aspected will show whether they like that or not.

Moon near the Descendent or in the 7th House may show as an assumption of being in relationship with everyone they are near to. Sometimes this person will forget to say anything to their companion due to not feeling the need. Other people may find this a bit offhand, but when anyone makes the effort to connect with this person, they find them immediately receptive.

☿ Mercury:

The House containing Mercury is the area of life that gets the spotlight of our conscious attention most. The issues of this House will be the subjects that provoke our thought, and we are therefore more likely to want to learn about them. As we think, so we communicate, and conversations are likely to come back to these areas. Where Mercury is, we want to understand, which tends to result in us focusing on the problems of that area.

Mercury in the 8th House shows a person with the mentality of a detective, always trying to get to the bottom of things. If the Mercury is in Taurus, the person will look at the depths in a practical way perhaps aiming to find a practical solution; if in Libra, they may be examining a situation with a view to establishing harmony.

In the 12th House, Mercury tends to think best when alone, which makes writing a comfortable way to communicate. Conscious understandings can arise from dreams, or in meditation, if the person is open to learning this way.

Venus: ♀

We tend to express our personal love in the area of the Venus House. We want to be in relationship in those specific activities, and we feel loved when people appreciate our efforts there. Because we are likely to express our lovelier behaviour there, we tend to receive more contact with people when we are involved in the activities of that House.

Venus in the 10th House will attract people when occupied with their career, in the 9th House, when travelling or studying their favourite subjects. With Venus in the 4th House, people will be attracted to their home, in the 12th House, the contacts can be more inner and often spiritual.

Uncomfortable aspects to Venus will show as relationship difficulties when the person is involved in the activities of the House: in the 6th House, a tendency to have trouble with colleagues, or maybe a health problem connected to the throat; in the 2nd House, perhaps recurring problems with those living in the same house and sharing possessions.

Whatever the House, the problems can be sorted out only by the person themselves working on understanding the principle of love. That love attracts and receives, it does not take or possess.

♂ Mars:

We tend to energise those situations that relate to the Mars House. Mars in the 7th House shows in dynamic relationships, in the 9th House, in the energetic pursuit of learning or travel, depending on the Sign and aspects.

When we looked at planets in Signs, one of the useful exercises was to check the position of Mars for clues to give us methods for triggering our energy when we need it. Using the Houses as well as Signs gives us more information, because the House placing of Mars shows the area of activity that that fires our energy for action.

For instance, Mars in the 5th House may show a person who needs to feel they have room to be creative; and when life becomes repetitive they will have no energy at all. To get energy flowing, they will need to discover or create an enjoyable side to the work.

However, Mars in the 6th House will simply find that the energy flows when work is there to be done. Mars in the 12th may find that they are better working on their own, whereas in the 7th they will need company every now and then to keep the flow going, even if that company is just a telephone call.

♃ Jupiter:

The House containing Jupiter will be an area where we grow and expand easily from an early age. If we are not engaged in any activity relating to this House, we will feel stunted and blocked, giving rise to depression or frustration or illness, whichever is our personal response. Activating the Jupiter House brings a breath of fresh air into our lives, with a sense of greater possibilities and a straightforward pleasure in life.

A person with Jupiter in the 12th House needs to be involved in some kind of inner work, where they will meet the Jupiter as a Guardian Angel energy; there will be great pleasure derived from time alone.

Jupiter in the 10th House may show a person who makes a career of their job by giving unstintingly, and their efforts will be reflected by an approving boss. It could also be a person daring to follow their vocation instead of steady employment, who then receives the gratitude of all those who benefit.

When we carry out, in any House containing Jupiter, those expansive activities where focus is on the activity rather than on ourselves doing it, Jupiter is reflected back to us as encouragement and opportunities to expand in the field of that House and any of the Houses connected to Jupiter by aspect.

Saturn: ♄

The House containing Saturn is that area of life where we feel a serious need to be in control; it is the same area where we received the discipline of authority figures in childhood. We are liable to blame the people relevant to that House for the testing times we have there, but many of the tests are difficult only if we have not been doing the necessary work beforehand. Once we accept that we are largely setting up our own difficulties, we come to understand what is really happening. The inner developmental work results in a wisdom and natural authority that other people will accept and appreciate.

For instance, Saturn in the 9th House shows first as a fairly rigid set of rules in childhood, an ideology that was expressed as a fixed truth. Later, this person will need to examine their assumptions about life, or they may continue to limit themselves in the same way their parents did. A person with a 9th House Saturn may well choose to follow a course of study which they would take very seriously, and eventually, because Saturn generally unfolds slowly in life, they could find themselves sharing the chosen subject with others. If they have been through the process of disciplining their own study and discovering their own truth, they could be good, patient teachers.

The early life of one with Saturn in the 3rd House will show some kind of restriction in spontaneous talking, possibly a difficult school life, or an absence of someone to talk to. Later, as they learn communication skills, they will need to accept that they sound authoritative when they speak, and they will naturally take responsibility for what they say.

If Saturn has any connection with the 5th House, it brings a perseverance to creativity that enables works of art to be manifested. This is particularly noticeable in the field of music because enormous application is required to succeed to any standard, but it is relevant to all serious artistic endeavour.

Outer Planets

♅ **Uranus** in a House shows us in what area of life a person will tend to feel trapped, and therefore behave in ways that result in a sense of freedom.

In the 6th House, it reflects a person who needs freedom in their working life, and if it is not part of their job, they may well keep changing employment or work for themselves. It is clear that the most suitable kind of work would need to include an amount of independent choice or the use of initiative, or even movement from place to place, depending on the Sign Uranus occupies and how it fits the rest of the chart.

We bring into our Uranus House an energy of excitement and the unexpected which other people are not sure how to handle. We avoid predictability in order to remain unattached. Maintaining a certain detachment in that area of life enables us to have flashes of insight into what is really happening.

Uranus in the 3rd House shows a person who may keep quiet much of the time, and then surprise everyone with words that may well be enlightening, or may simply be meant to shock.

♆

Neptune shows us that a person is particularly open in the area of the House it occupies and that psychic or spiritual connection is a possibility through these activities. The person can experience confusion in the matters of that House until they dedicate those activities to a higher purpose than simply the personal.

In the 1st House it shows a person who goes forward in life dissolving the form of what they approach. They need to see the essence within people and share in the oneness of spirit in order not to be swamped by the merging process.

To have Neptune near the IC or in the 4th House can feel like standing on sand as the tide comes in, very uncertain, vague and insecure, unless and until the person realises that they are very sensitive, spiritual people. In the same way that we need a steady chair to stand on to reach up and change a light bulb, we need to stand on a well rooted IC to reach for and achieve the MC, which is our ideal activity in the world. Once this person has made spirituality the cornerstone of their life, their foundations are secure as rock and all the rest of life becomes easier.

♇ **Pluto**, in its House position, shows the issues that seem most important. A person who has Pluto near the Ascendent or in the 1st House is one for whom all life feels intensely important. Their fear tends to attract powerful and difficult situations, and they incur a great deal of needless suffering in their endeavour to survive the dangers they perceive at every turn. Other people tend to find this attitude a bit worrying, so they often have to deal with their difficulties alone.

What they need to know is that life *is* that important but need not be that dangerous, that our spirit only ever presents us with what we can manage, and wants only for us to grow into a state where we can better enjoy life. Pluto in this position indicates that this person is capable of the great self-transformation that is required to let go of their fearful controlling. In such a climate of deep change, the people around them are also able to transform.

Pluto in the 10th or 11th Houses indicates a person who feels a need to change the world in some way. It will be attended by a fear of doing that, and consequently a manner that is so intense that they can easily attract opposition or rejection. But there are times and situations that call for such people to swing the changes in human behaviour.

⚷ **Chiron** in a House shows the activities we lack confidence to engage in right from childhood. It can be read as the wound we were born with, as though in a past life we died of it, and so it is often seen in a person as great vulnerability when they are involved with the concerns of the House it occupies.

In the 11th House, Chiron may show a person who would like to help society, their country, or a particular group. They may also feel that people will not trust them, will belittle or misunderstand their efforts, and so they will have experienced putdowns that were not necessarily intended. There is likely to be a lack of confidence which seems to others quite unfounded. As they come to realise that their input is often welcome and trusted because it is valuable, the desire to help overcomes their anxiety, and they become catalysts for healing in whatever way suits the Sign.

A person who has Chiron in the 7th House is one who is wounded in the area of partnership. Tending to be attracted to people who are going to hurt them even unwittingly, they need to realise that that person can also be hurt. As they stretch out to care for the other, relationships become the field of change and healing for both.

Ruling planets of 'empty' Houses

The concerns of a House trigger the flow of energy of the planet it contains, and that flow creates activity. When a House contains no planet, those concerns do not of themselves spark activity. The area in life that we tap for the energy to handle those activities will be the House containing the ruling planet of the Sign on the cusp, the beginning of the House.

To follow through:

1. Look for the Sign on the cusp of the House which you are studying; this Sign will show the attitude to that area.
2. Look for the House position of the planet ruling that Sign. That planet's Sign and House will show the supporting energy the person can use for the House you are studying.

For example, suppose you are wondering about family, and the Sign on the 4th House cusp is Virgo. This person's attitude to home and family will be reflected by Virgo, probably helpful but also cool and analytical; there is also likely to be a tendency for self-criticism which will affect their emotional security. Mercury is the ruler of Virgo and if, for example, it is in the 1st House, the person will tend to talk about their home, family and early life as soon as you meet them, which might very well help them understand their inner feelings. If Mercury was in Gemini, we would expect the flow of talking to be emphasised; the aspects to Mercury will show if this is a comfortable thing for them to do or not.

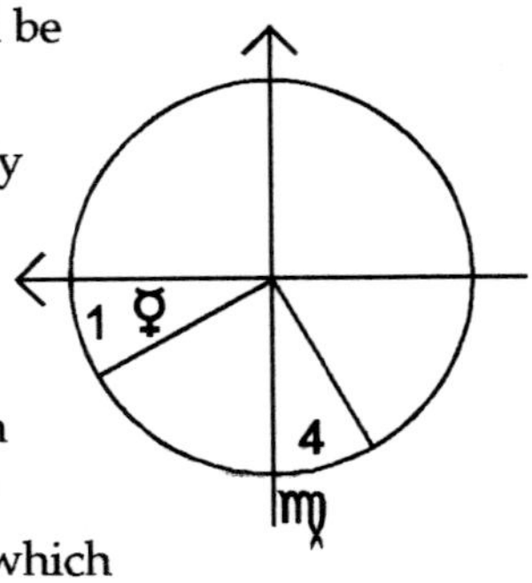

Again, imagine you are looking for the best kind of subject for a person to study, and you find Pisces on the cusp of the 9th House; you might say that the attitude to learning will be rather vague, unless they pursue spiritual or religious studies. If the ruler of Pisces, Neptune, is in the 11th House, they are more likely to feel attracted to a course if they would be studying with a group where they will be able feel a sense of bonding. Had that Neptune been in the 5th House, the subject they chose to study might well be more artistic and creative, and the studying just as comfortable on their own.

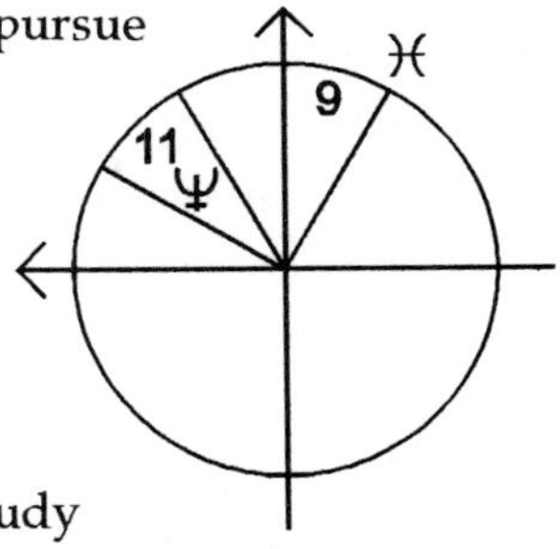

Looking at the 12th House, one might wonder what form of meditation would be most likely to appeal. If the cusp of the House is in Taurus, we might suggest meditating in nature, with trees, or the person imagining that they are a tree for strength and stability. If Venus, the ruler of Taurus, were in the 6th House, it might be easier and so more appropriate for the person to develop a meditative state when working. We would expect their work to involve relating to people (Venus) and they would feel more motivated to meditate (12th House) on behalf of their clients (6th House) for clarity and useful information.

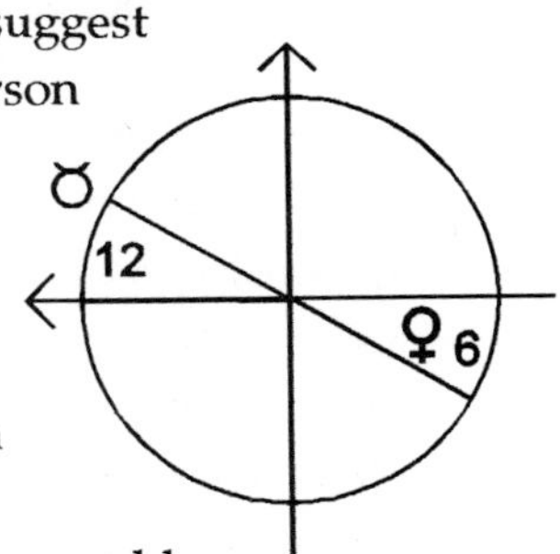

Exercise:

1. Take a House that interests you in your own or a friend's chart and look at the Sign on its cusp.
   What does that tell you about those issues or activities?
2. Find the position in the chart of the ruler of that Sign.
3. Expand your thinking about the original House to include the interests of the ruler's House.
4. Notice the difference.

Looking beyond the Windows

By now it should be clear that there is no cause to think that we know what makes someone tick, what moves them, what their priorities are. People are so complex that it would take years of patient study to cover all their character possibilities; and they are growing and changing all the time, whereas any piece of knowledge is static. Do we ever really know even our own personality? What is personality anyway? For each of us, our world is so personal, and yet we would like to know what is really out there.

The point of this questioning is to reach a state of not knowing who we all are, even our friends and family. In this way we are open to seeing each other as individuals who are a constantly changing surprise, and we will be nearer to true relating than any amount of knowledge could bring us. The study of their birth charts and our own gives us clues to those differences that we miss due to our unconscious assumptions: "Surely everyone is like that!" we say of some characteristic we take for granted in ourselves.

This study also helps us to approach a relationship difficulty or the struggle for a decision. One of the most valuable benefits of contact with one's birth chart is the confirmation of our feeling about ourselves, so that we are better able to accept our personality and not try to make it into something it cannot be. Perhaps, through that growing acceptance, we will become able to truly know ourselves in the greatest sense, and to encompass what is beyond our 'windows' on the world.

Chapter 5
Nodes of the Moon

Part 1
Ways in which we are the same

Our Story

The Nodes of the Moon seem to tell our story from before this life, through the present and into what we make of our potential. It is not that we leave our past behind; we never do that. We *are* our past; that is what we are made of, and so we bring it with us. The Nodes show how our ability to accept all that we are is the necessary first step towards the direction that attracts us. When going in that direction, there is a satisfaction that makes life feel worth living. We feel "That's what I want to be doing!" Even if we have difficulty with it, we still feel it is right for us. When we follow our own Nodal path, there is a feeling of determination and strength and rightness that goes beyond the everyday ups and downs of life.

The more we are aware of the oneness that we are in truth, the less we experience measurable time. Our spirit, pre-viewing this life, seeing the way things are and the processes and changes that will be happening in the world, recognises the appropriate time to be born. Scanning this life from that other dimension, looking for the time best suited to our arrival, we, as spirit, would consider what might be achievable in an earthly life, whether we could be helpful to the world, or learn to improve our own experience.

We may consider what attributes we are going to need from the many lifetimes we have lived before. If we had spent an entire lifetime working at building in certain attributes, an intuitive aspect of the imagination, for instance, or some practical skills, we would have become very good at them. In order to do this we would have needed to concentrate on a specific area of experience, and because we can't be aware of everything all the time, we would naturally have developed habits that enabled us to focus on that area. What we have been working on becomes a talent, a skill, so the habit patterns, stored in the unconscious, will kick in whenever the skill is next used.

We may have developed an infinite number of skills through many experiences, but we bring in only those that are relevant to this life. As it becomes clear which skills are relevant, we collect them and, along with them, come the old habits, attitudes, assumptions, and any unsolved problems left over from those lifetimes. These could include difficulties like a relationship that was not resolved, an accident that occurred when we were responsible, and maybe the end of that life where we had no time to integrate the experiences around that particular death.

Our chosen character manifests at our birth as a conglomerate of bits of personality, all described by the arrangement of the planets at the time. That group of personality tools is all to be combined and used in this life. In the chart, we look at the way the planets are linked together. Those planets that have a comfortable relationship with each other show the skills; and an uncomfortable relationship, shown by the presence of a difficult angle, indicates conflicting parts of ourselves. When astrologers are reading a birth chart they tend to see many different bits of character, all in the one person; we are all split personalities! During this life we endeavour to integrate the bits so that life is more pleasant.

As we come in, behind us is our past, a sense of what we understand and expect. While exactly opposite, in front of us, is the quality and area of life that calls us to achieve, not something specific, but rather an understanding or an expansion of our qualities. The past is represented by the South Node of the Moon, and our direction is towards the opposite point in the Zodiac, the North Node. If we are to speak of the Nodes without referring to past lives, we would say that the South Node shows what feels most natural to a person, what they expect.

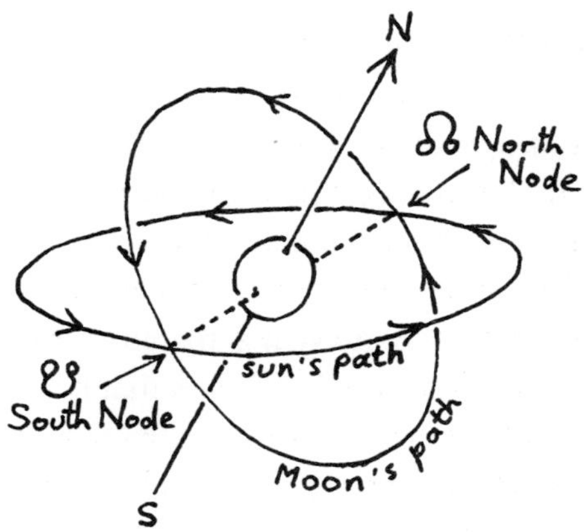

Astronomically speaking, we are looking from the Earth's point of view at the two great circles of the Sun and Moon. If you were to watch the Sun from the centre of the Earth, you would see it move through all the Signs of the Zodiac during a year, making a circle round the Earth, called 'the ecliptic'. The Moon's path takes only four weeks to complete and is at a different angle. Those two circles intersect at opposite points in the Zodiac called the Moon's Nodes with the Sun. Where the Moon was about to go South of the Sun's path is the South Node (☋), and the North Node (☊) is where the Moon was moving to the North of the Sun's path. Because the Moon represents the automatic personality, when contrasted with the Sun as the spirit, the Moon's Nodes speak to us of the role of the personality for the spirit.

The personality was gathered to do something in this life, and the Nodes give us a clue as to what that might be. They are sometimes called the Head and Tail of the Dragon, the person whose chart it is being the Dragon with their own Head facing the North Node and their Tail caught up in the South Node. It is as though we had a map of the land we have already explored, perhaps our last earthly experience before this life, shown by the Sign and House that contains our South Node. That kind of behaviour feels familiar and therefore gives a sense of security, even though it can create painful experiences.

In contrast, where we are going is unknown. We want to do that, or be there, but we tend to feel apprehensive or tentative about that area of our life (the House containing the North Node) and behaving in that way (its Sign). This is because it is the direction our spirit has chosen, and the personality senses that it will need to reach beyond itself to go that way. In the new land we have no map. Even though other people may find that kind of thing easy, we feel insecure there, no matter how much advice we get.

However, people often charge into life determined to go towards the North Node immediately, trying to do that Sign and House where the North Node falls in their chart, whenever they are feeling adventurous, or reckless. They manage it for a while but the lack of experience and skill in that area makes it is difficult to maintain. Things go wrong, mistakes are made, and the person tends to fall back into the South Node habits and assumptions because at least that is simple, even though not what they really want. Hopefully, we learn a little more at each attempt, understanding what is required of us as we improve contact with our spirit.

Off the path and getting back on

Sometimes, at an early age, people decide that the North Node area is too painful. They stop trying to achieve it and either carry on in the old ways which become less and less acceptable to them, or they lose their direction altogether.

Not being on one's Nodal path feels like being lost - "what am I here for?", "what am I supposed to be doing?". Nothing else that we attempt gives us that feeling of satisfaction. Inside we hold a sense of yearning that we may not even be able to define. When the North Node type of experience is spoken of, we feel "if only I could . . ." That longing can poison life.

The reason for this failure to achieve the North Node is that the tools we brought with us to do that job are on the step we came in on, shown by the South Node. To get back on the path it is necessary to look again at the South Node area of life to see what was important. We need to become aware of the habits that hold us back from development.

Habits of behaviour and attitude are areas of unconsciousness that need to be unlocked. They are just functions relevant to the past, and left to run on their own. Every now and then it is a good idea to check through our habits and bring them up to date, so that they are useful and do not hold us back. We need to correct our responses to situations so that they are appropriate in the moment.

We also need to respect ourselves for the abilities that we do have, rather than regarding them as universal and thinking that "surely everybody can do that", or even seeing them as weaknesses, as in the case of emotional sensitivity. Sometimes we have to relearn the skills or knowledge of the past, but we will always find that they come naturally, which suggests that we knew them before and are now remembering. All these are necessary tools to help us at every step.

It is also important to recognise that other people may not have our South Node abilities. When we use them only unconsciously, or for our own benefit, we lock ourselves into the personality, and the evolving force of life becomes uncomfortable; but if we use our South Node abilities to benefit others in whatever way feels natural to us, our spirit is expressed and our North Node expression attracts success.

The direction we are facing will be shown by the House and Sign that contain our North Node, the Head of our Dragon. It will be the best of that Sign that attracts us, and those ideals need to be held in mind like guiding stars, rather than as expectations of immediate achievement. As the South Node is sorted out, the untangling the Dragon's Tail, we find that the North Node activities and behaviour naturally unfold as long as we hold to those ideals. Our efforts to grow in this way attract the help we need to teach us how it is to be done. In a nutshell, when we have sorted out the step we are on, the next step appears of itself.

The twelve directions

The Nodes of the Moon travel backwards slowly through the Zodiac taking nineteen years to complete a cycle. In an Ephemeris, only the North Node position is given, the South Node being directly opposite. It is much more interesting to read about the Nodes if you know where they were when you and your friends were born, so this diagram shows the dates on which the North Node moved backwards from one Sign into the previous Sign. Only the month is given, so if your birth falls in one of the months mentioned, you will need to check in an Ephemeris, in a book shop perhaps, to check on which date the changeover happened.

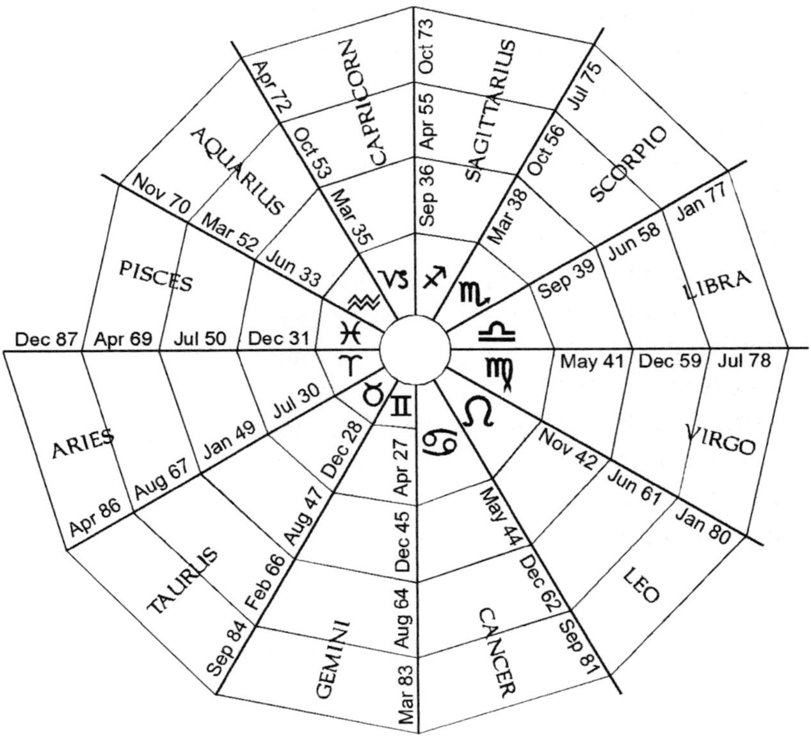

We will be looking at the Signs opposite to each other. The North Node is in the Sign and House that you came into earth 'facing', so you have behind you the Sign and House directly opposite.

☋ To describe the **South Node**, or where a person has 'come from', we will look for

1. *skills* and abilities of Sign and House, and
2. undermining *habits* of Sign and House.

☊ To describe the **North Node**, where and how a person wishes to be active, we will look for

1. the *ideals* of Sign and House, and
2. *mistakes* a beginner might make in that Sign and House.

☋♈ (♂) **South Node in Aries**: *(Ruler: Mars)*
Skills - independence, ability to take care of themselves, can operate on own initiative, good at knowing their own way:
habits - they never ask for help or company because they think no-one will help them, they assume they must 'go it alone'.

☊♎ (♀) Towards the **North Node in Libra**: *(Ruler: Venus)*
Ideal - to be in a relationship;
mistake - putting the other person first and forgetting to put their own side, which leads to frustration and finally pulling out of, or losing, the relationship.

What this person needs to remember is that they can manage on their own if necessary, and also that they *need* a little space to be themselves, so there is not the need to cling so hard to the relationship. They need to stop pushing people away as soon as relationship gets difficult. With a little more of the Aries courage, they will put their point of view as well as the partner's, for the Libran scales to balance. The conclusions reached will be less likely to frustrate them, and they will be nearer their Libran ideal of harmonious relationship.

South Node in Taurus: *(Ruler: Venus)* ☋♉ (♀)
Skills - feeling for the earth, steady and reliable, natural physical healing ability;
habits - stubborn fixity, thinking that time and silence heal problems.

Towards the **North Node in Scorpio**: *(Rulers: Pluto, Mars)* ☊♏ (♇♂)
Ideal - deep emotional understanding and connectedness;
mistake - stirring up emotions unnecessarily, and over-reacting.

This person needs to look towards their Taurus connection with nature, rather than towards their relationships, to give stability in their life. They will benefit from the silent acceptance of nature which will produce the steady, healed state that feels safe to them. From that basis they feel strong enough to speak of their hurt feelings gently and so attain more readily the Scorpio ideal of deep emotional sharing.

☋♊ **South Node in Gemini**: *(Ruler: Mercury)*
(☿) ***Skills*** - communication, ability to please by recognising and using other people's style and language;
habits - tendency to talk rather than listen so nothing is learned, being superficially pleasant and therefore not being trusted by others.

☊♐ Towards the **North Node in Sagittarius**:*(Ruler: Jupiter)*
(♃) ***Ideal*** - to understand the whole picture, to have an overview of life:
mistake - trying to talk about things not yet understood, settling for a superficial overview without the facts to base it on.

This person needs to listen with all their Gemini charm, in order to find the pieces that will go to make the Sagittarian picture of the whole. Speaking to people in the style they understand will draw those people out to speak of what interests them, and the philosophical breadth of conversation will come naturally.

☋♋ **South Node in Cancer**: *(Ruler: Moon)*
(☽) ***Skills*** - emotional sensitivity, a sense of what will nurture, of how to care for someone;
habits - identifying with the child-view of having no control in life, wanting to be cared for.

☊♑ Towards the **North Node in Capricorn**: *(Ruler: Saturn)*
(♄) ***Ideal*** - to be able to handle effectively any practical situation, to achieve practical aims.
mistake - taking responsibility for other people, instead of simply for themselves and their own experience.

This person is likely to feel that responsibility is too heavy for them and the result would be a sense of failure. They need to learn how to care for themselves, giving respect to their own emotional reactions. The caring they then give to others will be more understanding, coming from this position of growing strength. They become able to take on responsible positions without feeling small or emotionally overburdened.

South Node in Leo: *(Ruler: Sun)* ☋♌ (☉)
Skills - positive self-expression from the heart, ability to cheer others in times of hardship and stress;
habits - feeling defined by how others react to them, needing praise to feel good.

Towards the **North Node in Aquarius**: *(Rulers: Uranus, Saturn)* ☊♒ (♅♄)
Ideal - detached and accurate vision;
mistake - cutting off from other people which results in a lack of awareness of some important issues in situations, hence inaccuracy.

This is a person who is aiming at freedom and is likely to cut themselves off from others in the process. The result can be a kind of lifelessness. Their assumption is that they have to cheer everybody and be the centre that people want, when they are in company. It is indeed their good humour and cheerfulness that create their friendships, but where they give their true warm affection, people are happy to accept their unusualness and sudden changes, and they do have the freedom they seek. Their heartfelt sincerity wins them listeners no matter how 'off-the-wall' their ideas, and also gives them the courage to be different.

☋♍ (☿) **South Node in Virgo**: *(Ruler: Mercury)*
Skills - ability to see where change would improve experience, ability to recognise what is most useful, and what would be most helpful;
habits - criticizing automatically, too much self-criticism, perfectionism.

☊♓ (♆♃) Towards the **North Node in Pisces**: *Rulers: Neptune, Jupiter)*
Ideal - selfless service to humanity, strong intuitive/psychic ability;
mistake - fulfilling people's wishes rather than their needs, picking up everybody's feelings and suffering from them.

This person longs to merge with the things of the House which contains the Pisces North Node, but loses themselves in the emotional or psychic process. They need to focus on what they are doing, being precise and discriminating in their work for others. As they learn to stop beating themselves and everyone else into an idea of perfection that is not in the moment, and do their best to be helpful to anyone they meet, they find that they are one with humanity as a whole. As they work at being unemotionally conscious of the unseen world, they unfold their psychic gifts naturally.

☋♎ (♀) **South Node in Libra**: *(Ruler: Venus)*
Skills - diplomacy, the ability to see the many sides of an issue, knowing when action is called for and which action is right;
habits - refusing to act while omitting to consider the issue, being 'nice' rather than honest.

Towards the **North Node in Aries**: *(Ruler: Mars)* ☊♈
Ideal - knowing one's mind, fearless action in the right moment; (♂)
mistake - acting impulsively, managing alone.

This person desires to do things their own way, thereby finding themselves. It can seem to them that this is impossible in a relationship. Rather than trying to keep the peace, they need to use their diplomatic skills to express their truth and deal honestly with however the situation responds. They will find the courage to be themselves only through their work in relationship, because they need the response and support of another to define themselves.

South Node in Scorpio: *(Rulers: Pluto, Mars)* ☋♏
Skills - deep sensitivity to their own and others' emotions, determination and power to transform themselves; (♇♂)
habits - harbouring emotional reactions without sharing them, leading to vengeful behaviour.

Towards the **North Node in Taurus**: *(Ruler: Venus)* ☊♉
Ideal - to be steady, healthy and secure; (♀)
mistake - trying to support others before steadying themselves.

This person is coming down to earth and Nature will always be important to them. They aim to support others, being steady as a rock but others' emotions trigger their instability and they can let people down. When they have plumbed the memories in their own emotional depths, they find their bedrock at the bottom. This is then their stable base, and no story, however desperate, will be able to shake that foundation.

☊♊ (☿) **South Node in Sagittarius**: *(Ruler: Jupiter)*
Skills - ability to see the overview of any situation, natural philosophical understanding, ability to enthuse others;
habits - to withhold from explaining their thoughts, having fun at another's expense.

☋♐ (♃) Towards the **North Node in Gemini**: *(Ruler: Mercury)*
Ideal - to be able to communicate with anyone;
mistake - talking about trivialities where no-one is really interested.

This person can fall into chatting with people in a way that does not satisfy them. They need to be in touch with their natural philosophy so that their communications are interesting to them. The natural knowledge they are born with can be recognised by its obviousness when they first hear it. This person needs the attitude of putting their wisdom at people's service so that they communicate just that bit of the wider view that is relevant in the moment, and the satisfaction will be of discovering and encouraging everyone else's communication.

☋♑ (♄) **South Node in Capricorn**: *(Ruler: Saturn)*
Skills - able to handle responsibility well, competent and effective;
habits - expecting others to work as hard as themselves, allowing seriousness to become depression by not recognising their feelings.

☊♋ (☽) Towards the **North Node in Cancer**: (Ruler: Moon)
Ideal - to nurture the world through their caring;
mistake - holding on to those cared for, beyond usefulness.

This person needs to take responsibility for their own experiences in life rather than becoming overburdened by responsibility for others. Once they realise that everyone needs to take responsibility for themselves, they can turn their obvious abilities to teaching others with caring gentleness rather than doing things for them. They learn to support people emotionally through the learning process, allowing them to make their own mistakes and go their own way. They find then, that there is time to be playful, and even share children's light-hearted joy in life.

South Node in Aquarius: *(Rulers: Uranus, Saturn)* ☋♒ (♅♄)
Skills - ability to see clearly because of being detached;
habits - thinking that what is right for themselves must be right for everyone, not looking at their emotions.

Towards the **North Node in Leo**: *(Ruler: Sun)* ☊♌ (☉)
Ideal - to be oneself, to see the positive in every situation and person;
mistake - self-expression when not appropriate resulting in experiences of rejection.

This person needs to be in touch with who they are when on their own, so that they do not lose their centre by trying to appeal to 'the audience'. Being alone without connecting to their truth, will result in a hollow display when with others, but if they will go through the pain of opening their heart, their genuine inner light will inspire all they meet.

☋♓ (♆♃) **South Node in Pisces**: *(Rulers: Neptune, Jupiter)*
Skills - intuitive/psychic ability, empathising with all others;
habits - not limiting their psychic space which results in everyone being as affected by them, as they are affected by others.

☊♍ (☿) Towards the **North Node in Virgo**: *(Ruler: Mercury)*
Ideal - consciously working towards a better world for all;
mistake - thinking that there is one perfect way and that they know what it is.

This person needs their natural awareness of how others feel so that their ways of helping are appropriate to each person and situation. In their efforts to improve a situation, they can easily criticise the people which can have the reverse effect. When they focus on the impressions they have of the whole situation, they will find that they intuitively know the best thing to say or do.

Nodes of the Moon

Part 2

Ways in which we are different

The nodes, or intersection points, that the Moon's path makes with the Sun's path give us an axis across the chart drawn up for any moment. In a birth chart this axis can be interpreted as a direction which the person's spirit (Sun) gives to their personality (Moon) for this lifetime. There is, then, a sense of purpose or meaning to life when this direction is animated.

The style of a person's effort is developing from the South Node Sign alone to a combination of both Nodal Signs, and their personal priorities tend to be those of the North Node's House. The way to reach the satisfaction that is the keynote of travelling this direction, is to use the South Node abilities to give to others, keeping the North Node ideals as guides.

Ruling planets of the Nodes

Each Nodal Sign is ruled by a planet which, by its position in the chart gives more information about how that Node is working for the person, whether they find it easy or have many difficulties associated with its activity, whether it is in the forefront of their attention or working unconsciously in the background. The Nodal House is ruled by the planet ruling the Sign on the House Cusp which may be the same as the Nodal Sign. The House position of this planet gives us clues as to what activity, extra to the Nodal House itself, will activate the Node.

When the ruler of the South Node is in the North Node Sign, it perhaps indicates that the person is part way towards making the desired development; it is as though the energy that was used in the old activities has been redirected to align with the new ideals, and there is less pull back towards trying to be satisfied with the way things were.

The difficulty will be gathering the courage to use that energy in situations which are new and may seem daunting, especially as the planet will be weaker opposite its own rulership. For instance let us look at **South Node in Aries with Mars in the North Node Sign in Libra**; any habitual Aries aggression and thoughtlessness the person may feel will be tempered by a Libran consideration of others, which will be what the person wants to develop. But they may have difficulty getting their energy going and remembering that they can be independent. This difficulty will be emphasised if Mars conjuncts the North Node.

The ruler of the North Node in the South Node Sign perhaps indicates that there is much to balance and re-collect in the past, so that the alignment with the new direction will happen naturally when inner adjustments are made to situations that seem to recur. When the recurring reflection is recognised and accepted, the person will discover what attitude or assumption has been attracting it. Unhooking that thought from the unconscious releases energy which can then be used to help others.

For instance let us look at **Jupiter, as ruler of a Sagittarius North Node, in the South Node Sign, Gemini**. Here the expansive energy of Jupiter, which helps the person grow innerly so that they can see more of the whole picture, tends to be occupied with all kinds of ideas that

may distract them from their quest. Over and over they may find themselves too busy with disconnected activities to allow their ideas to develop. Perhaps they have been dependent on the praise they get for
doing things for others, so when they register this thought and drop the compulsive behaviour, they have the energy to communicate with real interest. The natural student/ teacher arises in them and the Sagittarian North Node is working.

Aspects to the Nodes

Aspects from planets to the Nodes indicate those parts of our personality that directly affect the unfolding of our path. They bring our growth or stagnation into daily importance. Often the Nodal path is unaspected. It will still be functioning as described but more as a background to life events. There will still be a sense of stuckness when we are off the path, and of satisfaction when we are on it, but not the emotional charge to either state.

Conjunction

A planet conjunct the South Node is an energy that ☌ ☋
we need to become aware of before our life will make sense. When the time comes in life to uncover the assumptions and regain the knowledge or skill, everything falls into place; our personal life will have meaning for us at last.

For instance, one way to interpret **Uranus conjunct the South Node** is that there may be some loss or separation in the past that may be more painful than the person wants to accept. Unless they accept it, the Uranian energy can be seen as cutting the entire experience out of their memory. If we refuse part of an old lifetime, we are unable to reclaim the skills we learned there. So the person rejecting this painful memory cannot use the skill of sensitivity that enabled them to feel the pain, even though that skill would help them deal with life. When this person retrieves the memory, they can then use the skill, and meaning comes back to life.

☌☊ A planet conjunct the North Node represents an energy that comes into play as soon as we align with our Nodal direction. We tend to feel this energy as a quality that does not belong to us. After the first effort to claim it, we become apprehensive about using that energy, because it seems that we are unable to maintain it. Other people seem to find that kind of behaviour easy and we doubt ourself because it seems so difficult for us in comparison. We look for people who can do it, projecting the energy onto them, and feeling ourselves incapable of being the way they are.

We will, of course, feel incomplete until we follow our Nodal direction and integrate the planetary energy connected with it, and the best way to do this is by deliberately sorting out the habits and collecting the abilities of the South Node. The ruler of the Sign containing the conjunction of North Node and planet will show a way in which one may overcome one's apprehension, through becoming involved with activities of its position in the chart.

For instance let us look at **Venus conjunct the North Node in Pisces**. This person may lack a sense of being able to relate well. Other people seem able to relate so much better, whereas they get lost trying to be what others want. This person has to go back to the Virgo South Node and rediscover their conscious focus, their ability to discriminate, in order to reclaim a self-contained point of view. Then they will be able to see what people really need, and the House containing Neptune, ruler of Pisces, will show in what activity they are best equipped to use their intuition to serve people well. This kind of relating will satisfy them more than simply trying to please.

Square

A planet square to both Nodes operates like a distraction from the Nodal path. We get into that energy and then feel stuck. It can feel like a conflict of interests, where we can see ourself getting in our own way. One way to look at it is that we need an extra ability on the path that is not directly linked with it, so we have to go 'off course' to learn it. When that work is done, we return to the path enriched. But there is a tendency to go off the path to the squaring planet whenever things get difficult, until the inner urge for growth drives us back again. Also there can be a sense that life 'disapproves' of the expression of that planetary energy, the style and preferred activities of that part of our nature.

It can be helpful to contemplate how that side of us actually assists our Nodal direction; we may discover that a **squaring Mars** represents the courage to delve into the past, and to face the unknown future, as long as we are not falling into negative use of energy. A **squaring Saturn**, while feeling like circumstances preventing our direction, can be stopping us from starting things too soon; if we hold to our course, accepting that it will take time and that there will be lessons to learn on the way, the Saturn will reflect our sense of steady determination, with which we can achieve almost anything.

Trine

A planet that trines one Node necessarily sextiles the other. When a planet trines the South Node it indicates a natural ability to use that planetary characteristic. For instance, **Jupiter trine the South Node** will indicate a natural generosity and openness that is part of our old skills. Sextile the North Node, this Jupiter quality will help us unfold our direction by attracting opportunities for growth that we can choose.

A planet trining the North Node represents an energy that helps us unfold our potential, encouraging us to keep going forward. It is a characteristic that gives us confidence to approach our future, its House indicating activities that will take us forward without our consciously trying. We may need to consciously focus this energy on the South Node area, in order to sort out what we are still bringing with us from the past. Otherwise we may rush into our direction, trailing and tripping over habits that are no longer appropriate. For instance, **Mercury trine the North Node** indicates a person who knows what their direction is and focuses their conscious thinking on that. They will probably need to deliberately search out their unconscious expectations in order to prevent themselves from recreating the past.

A personal path through life

Finding a person's direction in life gives a purpose for all their experiences, and a meaning for all their efforts. There are many ways of interpreting the Nodes in a birth chart, and it is extremely important that the direction as described should feel right to the person receiving it. Perhaps it is best to hint at what it might be and allow the person's own sense of joy and satisfaction to discover what it might truly be for themselves.

Their path through life is not only absolutely individual to a person, it is also subject to change, to unfolding, and even to complete transformation. It is a direction, not a goal that can be achieved, but there will be many satisfying achievements on the way. Once our feet are on that personal path, the spirit that we truly are is a constant companion, and all of life is lit with an inner confidence.

The Nodal axis is a direction that we face. In standing, as it were, on the rim of our experience, looking across the wheel of life to the other side, we are also facing the hub at the centre. Our effort to activate the North Node, while accepting all that we are in the South, draws us into the centre. In other words, we need only accept all that we are in the moment, in order to relax into the light that is in our centre, and radiate the spirit that we really are.

Conclusion

In essence, each person is one whole being, not divisible into parts. One whole cannot be divided into parts any more than that which is alive can be divided from the source of life. In complementary therapies, the 'whole person' is considered for treatment. In astrology, we also look at the whole person. But to do this, all systems appear to divide that person into spirit, mind, attitudes, emotions, body, direction, surroundings, and so on.

It is in order to speak about our experiences and our differences from each other, that we divide ourselves into many levels. So for example, we look at emotions independently from body even though they are two expressions of the same thing, the hormones being an obvious link, but also muscle tension, body posture, and so on.

Similarly, we divide spirit from mind, automatic reactions from considered responses, male from female behaviours, inner child from responsible adult, until we tend to feel like a chaotic assortment of bits and pieces that are impossible to integrate.

The essence that we are, which is expressed at so many different levels, cannot be wholly described from any one of them, and it is important to remember that all we are doing is describing the whole from many different perspectives, each view of limited value, and of no value at all unless seen as an aspect of the whole itself. The beauty of astrology is that its language is symbol and pattern, which can be read at any of the levels, giving us a sense of the unchanging essence.

It is the personality that has trouble, not the spirit: trouble with negative opposite Signs, difficult aspects between planets, anxiety about the North Node direction. The personality finds some Zodiac Signs difficult to understand, cannot see how they could possibly get on with others - but the spirit understands perfectly and dances with everything in the chart, with all the Zodiac Signs at once.

The centre of the circle

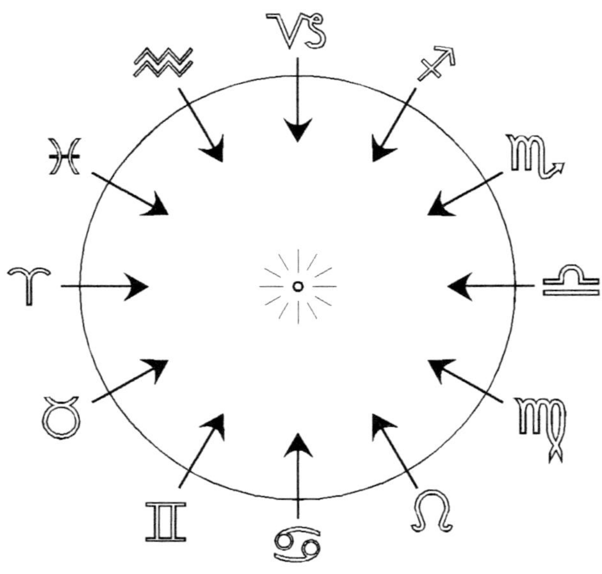

So, each of us contains the qualities of all twelve Signs, the energy of every planet, and the windows on life of all twelve Houses. Bearing this in mind, all twelve Nodal directions combine in every one of us.

As we look from the South Nodes towards the corresponding North Nodes, we are in fact facing across the centre, and it becomes a movement from outside to within: from the experiences we have of life, astrologically pictured round a circle as planets in Signs in Houses, to the point in the centre of the 'circle and cross' of our chart.

That centre point is the point of transformation where we fall through - into the truth of our eternal Oneness.

ABOUT THE AUTHOR

Margaret Koolman has been a practising astrologer for more than twenty years. She gives personal and postal readings to a worldwide clientele, and is also available for workshops.

Coming from a family with a background in theosophy and astrology, Margaret, who was born in the UK, was trained in the Western Mystery Tradition in London, before she moved on to specialise in astrology. In her astrological consultations she has developed a unique, understanding approach.

At present Margaret divides her time mainly between Hawai'i and the UK. She has a website at http://www.koolman.com, and can be contacted either

by phone to the UK - (+44) (0)1227-361623

or by e-mail - margaret@koolman.com

Further copies of this book may be obtained from good bookshops or the publisher at 14 Tyndale Park, Herne Bay, Kent CT6 6BP, UK.